101
COOKIE
RECIPES

A Collection of Your Favorites

PUBLICATIONS INTERNATIONAL, LTD.

Nutritional Analysis: The nutritional information that appears with certain recipes was submitted in part by the participating companies and associations. Every effort has been made to check the accuracy of these numbers. However, because numerous variables account for a wide range of values for certain foods, nutritive analyses in this book should be considered approximate.

Microwave Cooking: Microwave ovens vary in wattage. Use the cooking times as guidelines and check for doneness before adding more time.

101
COOKIE
RECIPES
A Collection of Your Favorites

Cookie

BAKING BASICS

Crisp or chewy, iced or spiced, filled or frosted, cookies are one of America's favorite foods to munch on. Whether you're baking for an after-school snack or preparing for a backyard picnic, use *101 Cookie Recipes* to make every kind of cookie, bar and brownie imaginable!

From melt-in-your-mouth simple cookies to beautiful holiday cookies, these easy-to-follow recipes are a delight to make, bake and eat. The following guidelines are chock-full of tips and hints for successful cookie baking. Be sure to read this section before you begin. Even the most accomplished bakers will discover helpful tips to make their time in the kitchen easier and more enjoyable.

Combine this useful information with over 101 kitchen-tested recipes developed by your favorite brand name food companies, and you have an impressive collection of cookie recipes to treasure for years to come.

Cookie Styles

The five basic cookie types include drop, bar, refrigerator, shaped and rolled. These types are determined by the consistency of the dough and how it is formed into cookies.

A **drop cookie** is as simple and easy as its name suggests—it is made by dropping spoonfuls of dough onto a cookie sheet. To get the number of cookies listed in a drop cookie recipe, drop cookie dough with a tableware spoon, not a measuring spoon.

Bar cookies are created by spooning batter or soft dough into a shallow pan, then baking and cutting the cooled cookie into bars. For variety, cut bar cookies into triangles or diamonds.

Refrigerator cookies (also called slice-and-bake cookies) are made by shaping the dough into a log, which is refrigerated until firm, then sliced and baked. The edges can be decorated by rolling the log in sprinkles or nuts before slicing.

A **shaped cookie** is formed by shaping dough by hand into small balls, logs, crescents and other shapes. These cookies can then be decorated before baking—rolled in sugar, filled with jam, topped with candies or flattened with a fork.

Rolled cookies are made by using a rolling pin to roll the dough out flat. Then cookies are cut into decorative shapes with cookie cutters. These cookies can be decorated with sprinkles prior to baking, or frosted after cooling.

Measuring Ingredients

Dry Ingredients: Always use standardized measuring spoons and cups. Fill the appropriate measuring spoon or cup to overflowing and level it off with a metal spatula or knife.

When measuring flour, lightly spoon it into the measuring cup and then level it off. Do not tap or bang the measuring cup since this will pack the flour. If a recipe calls for "sifted flour," sift the flour before it is measured. If a recipe calls for "flour, sifted," measure the flour first and then sift.

Liquid Ingredients: Use a standardized glass or plastic measuring cup with a pouring spout. Place the cup on a flat surface, fill to the desired mark and check the measurement at eye level. To make sure that sticky substances, like honey and molasses won't cling to the measuring cup, grease the cup or spray it with non-stick cooking spray before filling.

Melting Chocolate

Make sure the utensils used for melting chocolate are completely dry. Moisture causes chocolate to "seize," which means it becomes stiff and grainy. If this happens, add ½ teaspoon shortening (not butter) for each ounce of chocolate and stir until smooth. Chocolate scorches easily, and once scorched cannot be used. Follow one of these three methods for perfectly melted chocolate:

Double Boiler: This is the safest method because it prevents scorching. Place the chocolate in the top of a double boiler or in a bowl over hot (not boiling) water; stir until smooth. (Make sure that the water remains just below a simmer and is one inch below the bottom of the top pan.) Be careful that no steam or water gets into the chocolate.

Direct Heat: Place the chocolate in a heavy saucepan and melt over very low heat, stirring constantly. Remove the chocolate from heat as soon as it is melted. Be sure to watch the chocolate carefully because it is easily scorched when using this method.

Microwave Oven: Place an unwrapped 1-ounce square or 1 cup of chips in a small microwavable bowl. Microwave on HIGH (100% power) 1 to 1½ minutes, stirring after 1 minute. Stir the chocolate at 30-second intervals until smooth. Be sure to stir microwaved chocolate since it may retain its original shape even when melted.

Toasting & Tinting Techniques

Toasting Nuts: Toasting nuts brings out their flavor and fragrance. Spread the nuts in a single layer on a cookie sheet. Bake in a preheated 325°F oven for 8 to 10 minutes or until golden, stirring occasionally to ensure even toasting. The nuts will darken and become crisper as they cool.

Toasting Coconut: Spread the flaked coconut out in a thin layer on a cookie sheet. Bake in a preheated 325°F oven for 7 to 10 minutes. Shake the pan or stir the coconut occasionally during baking to promote even browning and prevent burning.

Tinting Coconut: Dilute a few drops of food coloring with

½ teaspoon milk or water in a small bowl. Add 1 to 1⅓ cups flaked coconut and toss with a fork until evenly tinted.

Mixing and Baking the Best Cookies

The real trick to scrumptious cookies is in the baking. Be sure to read the following baking instructions for sensational results.

• Read the entire recipe before you begin to be sure you have all the necessary ingredients.

• Butter and margarine are interchangeable only if both are listed in the ingredient list. Do not use low-fat spreads, soft or tub margarine unless the recipe specifically calls for these ingredients. They act differently and may produce unsatisfactory results.

• Toast and chop nuts, peel and slice fruit and melt chocolate before preparing the cookie dough.

• Shiny pans and cookie sheets are preferred for baking cookies and bars since they reflect heat and will produce light, delicate crusts.

• Grease cookie sheets only when the recipe recommends it, otherwise the cookies may spread too much. When making bar cookies, use the pan size recommended in the recipe.

• Bake cookies on the middle rack of the oven, one cookie sheet at a time. Uneven browning can occur if baking on more than one rack at a time.

• Cool cookie sheets completely before putting more cookie dough on them. Dropping cookie dough on warm cookie sheets causes excess spreading.

Storing and Freezing

Most cookie dough and cookies can be made ahead and stored or frozen for future use. The type of storage required depends upon the type of cookie you are making.

• Unbaked cookie dough can be refrigerated for up to one week or frozen for up to six weeks. Rolls of dough (for refrigerator cookies) should be sealed tightly in plastic wrap; other doughs should be stored in airtight containers. Label dough or container with baking information for convenience.

• Keep soft cookies in airtight containers. If they begin to dry out, add a piece of apple or bread to the container to help cookies retain moisture. Be sure to store soft and crisp cookies separately.

• Store crisp cookies in containers with loose-fitting lids to prevent moisture buildup. If they become soggy, heat undecorated cookies in a preheated 300°F oven for 3 to 5 minutes to restore crispness.

• Store cookies with sticky glazes, fragile decorations and icings in single layers between waxed paper.

• As a rule, crisp cookies freeze better than soft, moist cookies. Rich, buttery bar cookies are an exception since they freeze exceptionally well. Freeze baked cookies in airtight containers or freezer bags for up to six months. Thaw cookies and brownies unwrapped at room temperature. Meringue-based cookies *do not* freeze well and chocolate-dipped cookies will discolor if frozen.

Sending Cookies

Bake soft, moist cookies that can handle jostling rather than fragile, brittle cookies that might crumble. Brownies and bar cookies are generally sturdy, but avoid shipping those with moist fillings and frostings since they become sticky at room temperature. Shipping anything with chocolate during the summer or in warm climates is also risky business.

Wrap each type of cookie separately to retain flavors and textures. Cookies can also be wrapped back-to-back in pairs with either plastic wrap or foil. Bar cookies should be packed in layers the size of the container, or they can be sent in a covered foil pan as long as the pan is well-cushioned inside the shipping box. Place wrapped cookies as tightly as possible in snug rows inside a sturdy box or container.

Fill the bottom of the shipping box with an even layer of packing material. Do not use popped popcorn or puffed cereal as it may attract insects. Place another layer of packing material between layers of wrapped cookies. Fill any crevices and add a final layer of packing material to the top of the box. Ship the container to arrive as soon as possible.

Fabulous Final Touches

A few extra minutes spent on easy decorations can add eye-appeal. Try any of the following ideas to jazz up your cookies and brownies.

Chocolate for Dipping: Nothing makes a cookie stand out more than being partially or completely dipped in chocolate! Simply dip cookies in melted chocolate (milk, dark, white or some of each) and place on waxed paper until the chocolate is set.

Chocolate for Drizzling: Use a spoon or fork to drizzle melted chocolate over cookies, bars and brownies. Or, melt chocolate in a small resealable plastic freezer bag, cut off a very tiny corner of the bag and squeeze out the chocolate in patterns or designs over the cookies.

Nuts: Whole, halved, chopped and sliced nuts can add extra flavor and texture to all types of cookies. Try using nuts in combination with a white or chocolate drizzle for an eye-catching, irresistible topping.

Colored Sugar, Sprinkles and Candies: These decorations are simple and fun to use to dress up an ordinary cookie. Best of all, they are bright and colorful to attract attention.

Creative Cookie Presentation

For your next birthday party or celebration, use cookies to create cute party foods. Kids will love to eat these fun treats!

Cookie Lollipops: Before baking, push ice cream sticks into balls of cookie dough. Flatten dough ball with your hand to form a round lollipop. Bake as recipe directs.

Cookie Ice Cream Sandwiches: Turn your favorite chocolate chip cookies into frozen treats! Simply assemble cookies in pairs with about 1/3 cup softened ice cream; press cookies together lightly. Wrap each sandwich in plastic wrap; freeze until firm.

Cookie Sundaes: Add cookies or brownies to a bowl with ice cream to create a rich dessert.

Cheery

COOKIE JAR
FAVORITES

Crispy Oat Drops

1 cup (2 sticks) butter or margarine,
    softened
½ cup granulated sugar
½ cup firmly packed light brown sugar
1 large egg
2 cups all-purpose flour
½ cup quick-cooking or old-fashioned oats,
    uncooked
1 teaspoon cream of tartar
½ teaspoon baking soda
¼ teaspoon salt
1¾ cups "M&M's"® Semi-Sweet Chocolate
    Mini Baking Bits
1 cup toasted rice cereal
½ cup shredded coconut
½ cup coarsely chopped pecans

Preheat oven to 350°F. In large bowl cream butter and sugars until light and fluffy; beat in egg. In medium bowl combine flour, oats, cream of tartar, baking soda and salt. Blend flour mixture into creamed mixture. Stir in "M&M's"® Semi-Sweet Chocolate Mini Baking Bits, cereal, coconut and pecans. Drop by heaping tablespoonfuls about 2 inches apart onto ungreased cookie sheets. Bake 10 to 13 minutes or until lightly browned. Cool completely on wire racks. Store in tightly covered container.

Makes about 4 dozen cookies

Crispy Oat Drops

Irresistible Peanut Butter Cookies

1¼ cups firmly packed light brown sugar
¾ cup creamy peanut butter
½ CRISCO® Stick or ½ cup CRISCO®
    all-vegetable shortening
3 tablespoons milk
1 tablespoon vanilla
1 egg
1¾ cups all-purpose flour
¾ teaspoon baking soda
¾ teaspoon salt

1. Heat oven to 375°F. Place sheets of foil on countertop for cooling cookies.

2. Combine brown sugar, peanut butter, shortening, milk and vanilla in large bowl. Beat at medium speed of electric mixer until well blended. Add egg. Beat just until blended.

3. Combine flour, baking soda and salt. Add to creamed mixture at low speed. Mix just until blended.

4. Drop by rounded measuring tablespoonfuls of dough 2 inches apart onto ungreased baking sheet. Flatten slightly in crisscross pattern with tines of fork.

5. Bake one baking sheet at a time at 375°F for 7 to 8 minutes, or until set and just beginning to brown. *Do not overbake.* Cool 2 minutes on baking sheet. Remove cookies to foil to cool completely.   *Makes about 3 dozen cookies*

Oatmeal Scotchies™

1¼ cups all-purpose flour
1 teaspoon baking soda
½ teaspoon salt
½ teaspoon ground cinnamon
1 cup (2 sticks) butter or margarine,
    softened
¾ cup granulated sugar
¾ cup packed brown sugar
2 eggs
1 teaspoon vanilla extract *or* grated peel of
    1 orange
3 cups quick or old-fashioned oats
1⅔ cups (11-ounce package) NESTLÉ®
    TOLL HOUSE® Butterscotch Flavored
    Morsels

COMBINE flour, baking soda, salt and cinnamon in small bowl. Beat butter, granulated sugar, brown sugar, eggs and vanilla extract in large mixer bowl. Gradually beat in flour mixture. Stir in oats and morsels. Drop by rounded tablespoon onto ungreased baking sheets.

BAKE in preheated 375°F. oven for 7 to 8 minutes for chewy cookies; 9 to 10 minutes for crisp cookies. Cool on baking sheets for 2 minutes; remove to wire racks to cool completely.   *Makes about 4 dozen cookies*

Oatmeal Scotchie™ Pan Cookies: SPREAD dough into greased 15½×10½-inch jelly-roll pan. Bake in preheated 375°F. oven for 18 to 22 minutes or until very lightly browned. Cool completely on wire rack. Makes 4 dozen bars.

Irresistible Peanut Butter Cookies

Double Chocolate Cherry Cookies

COOKIES

1½ cups firmly packed light brown sugar
⅔ CRISCO® Stick or ⅔ cup CRISCO® all-vegetable shortening
1 tablespoon water
1 teaspoon vanilla
2 eggs
1½ cups all-purpose flour
⅓ cup unsweetened cocoa powder
½ teaspoon salt
¼ teaspoon baking soda
30 to 40 maraschino cherries

ICING

½ cup semisweet chocolate chips or white chocolate chips
½ teaspoon CRISCO® stick or CRISCO® all-vegetable shortening

1. Heat oven to 375°F. Place sheets of foil on countertop for cooling cookies.

2. For cookies, place brown sugar, shortening, water and vanilla in large bowl. Beat at medium speed of electric mixer until well blended. Add eggs; beat well.

3. Combine flour, cocoa, salt and baking soda. Add to shortening mixture; beat at low speed just until blended.

4. Shape rounded measuring tablespoonfuls of dough around each maraschino cherry, covering cherry completely. Place cookies 2 inches apart on ungreased baking sheet.

5. Bake one baking sheet at a time for 7 to 9 minutes or until cookies are set. *Do not overbake.* Cool 2 minutes on baking sheet. Remove cookies to foil to cool completely.

6. For icing, place chocolate chips and shortening in heavy resealable sandwich bag; seal bag. Microwave at 50% (MEDIUM) for 1 minute. Knead bag. If necessary, microwave at 50% power another 30 seconds at a time until mixture is smooth when bag is kneaded. Cut a small tip off corner of bag; drizzle chocolate over cookies.

Makes about 3 dozen cookies

Fruit Burst Cookies

1 cup margarine or butter, softened
¼ cup sugar
1 teaspoon almond extract
2 cups all-purpose flour
½ teaspoon salt
1 cup finely chopped nuts
SMUCKER'S® Simply Fruit

Preheat oven to 400°F. Beat margarine and sugar in large bowl until light and fluffy. Blend in almond extract. Combine flour and salt in large bowl; add to margarine mixture and beat well.

Shape level tablespoonfuls of dough into balls; roll in nuts. Place 2 inches apart on ungreased cookie sheets; flatten slightly. Make small indentation in centers of cookies; fill with fruit spread.

Bake for 10 to 12 minutes or just until lightly browned. Cool. *Makes 2½ dozen cookies*

Double Chocolate Cherry Cookies

Double Chocolate Sugar Cookies

2 egg whites, slightly beaten
¼ cup (½ stick) vegetable oil spread
    (60% oil), melted
1 tablespoon water
1 teaspoon vanilla extract
2½ cups HERSHEY'S Basic Cocoa Baking
    Mix (recipe follows)
¼ cup sugar
    Chocolate Glaze (recipe follows)

Heat oven to 350°F. Lightly spray cookie sheet with vegetable cooking spray. In medium bowl, stir together egg whites, corn oil spread, water and vanilla. Stir in Basic Cocoa Baking Mix until well blended. Shape dough into 1-inch balls. Roll in sugar to coat. Place 2 inches apart on prepared cookie sheet. Press balls flat with bottom of glass.

Bake 6 to 8 minutes or until set. Cool 5 minutes; remove from cookie sheet to wire rack. Cool completely. Drizzle Chocolate Glaze over tops of cookies. Let stand until set. Store, covered, at room temperature.   *Makes 2½ dozen cookies*

Hershey's Basic Cocoa Baking Mix: Stir together 4½ cups all-purpose flour, 2¾ cups sugar, 1¼ cups HERSHEY'S Cocoa, 1 tablespoon plus ½ teaspoon baking powder, 1¾ teaspoons salt and 1¼ teaspoons baking soda. Store in airtight container in cool, dry place for up to 1 month. Stir before using. Makes 8 cups mix.

Chocolate Glaze: In small microwave-safe bowl, place ¼ cup HERSHEY'S Semi-Sweet Chocolate Chips and ½ teaspoon shortening (do not use butter, margarine or oil). Microwave at HIGH (100%) 30 seconds; stir. If necessary, microwave at HIGH an additional 30 seconds or until chips are melted and mixture is smooth when stirred. Use immediately.

Nutrients per Serving (2 cookies with glaze):

Calories: 70, Total Fat: 3.5 g, Cholesterol: 0 mg, Sodium: 170 mg

Cinnamon-Apricot Tart Oatmeal Cookies

⅓ cup water
1 package (6 ounces) dried apricot halves,
    diced
1¼ cups firmly packed brown sugar
¾ Butter Flavor* CRISCO® Stick or ¾ cup
    Butter Flavor* CRISCO® all-vegetable
    shortening
1 egg
⅓ cup milk
1½ teaspoons vanilla
3 cups quick oats, uncooked
1 cup all-purpose flour
½ teaspoon baking soda
½ teaspoon salt
¼ teaspoon cinnamon
1 cup plus 2 tablespoons chopped pecans

*Butter Flavor Crisco is artificially flavored.

1. Place ⅓ cup water in small saucepan. Heat to a boil over high heat. Place diced apricots in strainer over boiling water. Reduce heat to low. Cover; cook 15 minutes. Set aside.

2. Heat oven to 375°F. Grease baking sheets with shortening. Place sheets of foil on countertop for cooling cookies.

3. Combine brown sugar, shortening, egg, milk and vanilla in large bowl. Beat at medium speed of electric mixer until well blended.

4. Combine oats, flour, baking soda, salt and cinnamon. Mix into shortening mixture at low speed until just blended. Stir in pecans, apricots and liquid from apricots.

5. Drop dough by rounded measuring tablespoonfuls 2 inches apart onto prepared baking sheet.

6. Bake one baking sheet at a time for 10 to 12 minutes or until lightly browned. *Do not overbake.* Cool 2 minutes on baking sheets. Remove cookies to foil to cool completely.

Makes 3½ to 4 dozen cookies

Double Chocolate Cookies

2¼ cups all-purpose flour
1 teaspoon baking soda
1 teaspoon salt
1 cup (2 sticks) butter or margarine, softened
¾ cup granulated sugar
¾ cup firmly packed brown sugar
1 teaspoon vanilla extract
2 eggs
2 (2-ounce) envelopes NESTLÉ® Choco-Bake® Unsweetened Baking Chocolate Flavor
2 cups (12-ounce package) NESTLÉ® TOLL HOUSE® Semi-Sweet Chocolate Morsels
1 cup chopped walnuts

COMBINE flour, baking soda and salt in small bowl. Beat butter, granulated sugar, brown sugar and vanilla in large mixer bowl. Beat in eggs and Choco-Bake. Gradually beat in flour mixture. Stir in morsels and nuts. Drop by rounded tablespoons onto ungreased baking sheets.
BAKE in preheated 375°F oven for 8 to 10 minutes or until edges are set but centers are still slightly soft. Let stand for 2 minutes; remove to wire racks to cool completely.

Makes about 6 dozen (2½-inch) cookies

Pinwheel Cookies

½ Butter Flavor* CRISCO® Stick or ½ cup
   Butter Flavor* CRISCO® all-vegetable
   shortening
⅓ cup plus 1 tablespoon butter, softened and
   divided
2 egg yolks
½ teaspoon vanilla
1 package DUNCAN HINES® Moist
   Deluxe Fudge Marble Cake Mix

*Butter Flavor Crisco is artificially flavored.

1. Combine shortening, ⅓ cup butter, egg yolks
and vanilla in large bowl. Mix at low speed of
electric mixer until blended. Set aside cocoa
packet from cake mix. Gradually add cake mix.
Blend well.

2. Divide dough in half. Add cocoa packet and
remaining 1 tablespoon butter to one half of
dough. Knead until well blended and chocolate
colored.

3. Roll out yellow dough between two pieces of
waxed paper into 18×12×⅛-inch rectangle.
Repeat for chocolate dough. Remove top pieces
of waxed paper from chocolate and yellow dough.
Lay yellow dough directly on top of chocolate.
Remove remaining layers of waxed paper. Roll up
jelly roll fashion, beginning at wide side.
Refrigerate 2 hours.

4. Preheat oven to 350°F. Grease cookie sheets.
Cut dough into ⅛-inch slices. Place sliced dough
1 inch apart on prepared cookie sheets. Bake 9 to
11 minutes or until lightly browned. Cool 5
minutes on cookie sheets. Remove to cooling
racks.   *Makes about 3½ dozen cookies*

Peanut Butter Chip Oatmeal Cookies

1 cup (2 sticks) butter or margarine,
   softened
¼ cup shortening
2 cups packed light brown sugar
1 tablespoon milk
2 teaspoons vanilla extract
1 egg
2 cups all-purpose flour
1⅔ cups (10-ounce package) REESE'S®
   Peanut Butter Chips
1½ cups quick-cooking or regular rolled oats
½ cup chopped walnuts
½ teaspoon baking soda
½ teaspoon salt

Heat oven to 375°F. In large mixer bowl, beat
butter, shortening, brown sugar, milk, vanilla and
egg until light and fluffy. Add remaining
ingredients; mix until well blended. Drop dough
by rounded teaspoonfuls about 2 inches apart
onto ungreased cookie sheets. Bake until light
brown, 10 to 12 minutes for soft cookies or 12 to
14 minutes for crisp cookies. Remove from cookie
sheets to wire rack. Cool completely.
                    Makes about 6 dozen cookies

Pinwheel Cookies

Soft Apple Cider Cookies

1 cup firmly packed light brown sugar
½ cup margarine, softened
½ cup apple cider
½ cup EGG BEATERS® Healthy Real Egg
    Substitute
2¼ cups all-purpose flour
1½ teaspoons ground cinnamon
1 teaspoon baking soda
¼ teaspoon salt
2 medium apples, peeled and diced
    (about 1½ cups)
¾ cup almonds, chopped
    Cider Glaze (recipe follows)

In large bowl, with electric mixer at medium speed, beat sugar and margarine until creamy. Add cider and Egg Beaters®; beat until smooth. With electric mixer at low speed, gradually blend in flour, cinnamon, baking soda and salt. Stir in apples and almonds.

Drop dough by tablespoonfuls, 2 inches apart, onto greased baking sheets. Bake at 375°F for 10 to 12 minutes or until golden brown. Remove from sheets; cool on wire racks. Drizzle with Cider Glaze.   *Makes 4 dozen cookies*

Cider Glaze: In small bowl, combine 1 cup powdered sugar and 2 tablespoons apple cider until smooth.

Prep Time: 30 minutes

Cook Time: 12 minutes

Nutrients per Serving (1 cookie):

Calories: 80, Total Fat: 3 g, Cholesterol: 0 mg, Sodium: 80 mg

Traditional Oat and Raisin Cookies

1 cup vegetable shortening
1 cup granulated sugar
1 cup packed brown sugar
2 eggs
1 teaspoon vanilla extract
1½ cups all-purpose flour
1 teaspoon baking soda
1 teaspoon ground cinnamon
¼ teaspoon ground nutmeg
3 cups quick or old-fashioned oats
1 cup raisins

Preheat oven to 350°F. Lightly grease cookie sheet. Beat shortening, granulated and brown sugars until creamy. Add eggs and vanilla; beat well. Combine flour, baking soda, cinnamon, nutmeg and salt, if desired; mix well. Add to shortening mixture; mix well. Stir in oats and raisins; mix well. Drop by rounded teaspoons onto prepared cookie sheet.

Bake 10 to 12 minutes or until golden brown. Let stand 1 minute; cool completely on wire racks.
                    Makes 5 dozen cookies

Soft Apple Cider Cookies

Marbled Biscotti

½ cup (1 stick) butter or margarine, softened
1 cup granulated sugar
2 large eggs
1 teaspoon vanilla extract
2½ cups all-purpose flour
1 teaspoon baking powder
1 teaspoon baking soda
1¾ cups "M&M's"® Chocolate Mini Baking Bits, divided
1 cup slivered almonds, toasted*
¼ cup unsweetened cocoa powder
2 tablespoons instant coffee granules

*To toast almonds, spread in single layer on baking sheet. Bake at 350°F for 7 to 10 minutes until light golden, stirring occasionally. Remove almonds from pan and cool completely before using.

Preheat oven to 350°F. Lightly grease cookie sheets; set aside. In large bowl cream butter and sugar until light and fluffy; beat in eggs and vanilla. In medium bowl combine flour, baking powder and baking soda; blend into creamed mixture. Dough will be stiff. Stir in 1¼ cups "M&M's"® Chocolate Mini Baking Bits and nuts. Divide dough in half. Add cocoa powder and coffee granules to half of the dough, mixing to blend. On well-floured surface, gently knead doughs together just enough to marble. Divide dough in half and gently roll each half into 12×2-inch log; place on prepared cookie sheets at least 4 inches apart. Press remaining ½ cup "M&M's"® Chocolate Mini Baking Bits onto outside of both logs. Bake 25 minutes. Dough will spread. Cool logs 15 to 20 minutes. Slice each log into 12 slices; arrange on cookie sheet cut-side down. Bake an additional 10 minutes. (For softer biscotti, omit second baking.) Cool completely. Store in tightly covered container.

Makes 24 pieces

Lemony Butter Cookies

½ cup butter, softened
½ cup sugar
1 egg
1½ cups all-purpose flour
1 teaspoon grated lemon peel
2 tablespoons fresh lemon juice
½ teaspoon baking powder
⅛ teaspoon salt
Additional sugar

Beat butter and sugar in large bowl with electric mixer until creamy. Beat in egg until light and fluffy. Mix in flour, lemon peel and juice, baking powder and salt. Cover; refrigerate about 2 hours or until firm.

Preheat oven to 350°F. Roll out dough, a small portion at a time, on well-floured surface to ¼-inch thickness. (Keep remaining dough in refrigerator.) Cut with 3-inch round cookie cutters. Transfer to ungreased cookie sheets. Sprinkle with sugar.

Bake 8 to 10 minutes or until lightly browned on edges. Cool 1 minute on cookie sheets. Remove to wire racks; cool completely.

Makes about 2½ dozen cookies

Marbled Biscotti

Peanut Butter Cut-Out Cookies

1 cup REESE'S® Peanut Butter Chips
½ cup butter or margarine
⅔ cup packed light brown sugar
1 egg
¾ teaspoon vanilla extract
1⅓ cups all-purpose flour
½ cup finely chopped pecans
¾ teaspoon baking soda
Chocolate Chip Glaze (recipe follows)

In medium saucepan, place peanut butter chips and butter; cook over low heat, stirring constantly, until melted. Pour into large bowl; add brown sugar, egg and vanilla, beating until well blended. Stir in flour, pecans and baking soda blending well. Refrigerate 15 to 20 minutes or until firm enough to roll.

Preheat oven to 350°F. Roll a small portion of dough at a time on lightly floured board, or between 2 pieces of waxed paper to ¼-inch thickness. (Keep remaining dough in refrigerator.) With cookie cutters, cut dough into desired shapes; place on ungreased cookie sheets. Bake 7 to 8 minutes or until almost set (do not overbake). Cool 1 minute; remove from cookie sheets to wire racks. Cool completely. Drizzle Chocolate Chip Glaze onto each cookie; allow to set.   *Makes about 3 dozen cookies*

Chocolate Chip Glaze: In top of double boiler over hot (not boiling) water melt 1 cup HERSHEY'S® Semi-Sweet Chocolate Chips with 1 tablespoon shortening; stir until smooth. Remove from heat; cool slightly, stirring occasionally.

Gingersnaps

2½ cups all-purpose flour
1½ teaspoons ground ginger
1 teaspoon baking soda
1 teaspoon ground allspice
½ teaspoon salt
1½ cups sugar
2 tablespoons margarine, softened
½ cup MOTT'S® Apple Sauce
¼ cup GRANDMA'S® Molasses

1. Preheat oven to 375°F. Spray cookie sheet with nonstick cooking spray.

2. In medium bowl, sift together flour, ginger, baking soda, allspice and salt.

3. In large bowl, beat sugar and margarine with electric mixer at medium speed until blended. Whisk in apple sauce and molasses.

4. Add flour mixture to apple sauce mixture; stir until well blended.

5. Drop rounded tablespoonfuls of dough 1 inch apart onto prepared cookie sheet. Flatten each slightly with moistened fingertips.

6. Bake 12 to 15 minutes or until firm. Cool completely on wire rack.

Makes 3 dozen cookies

Peanut Butter Cut-Out Cookies

Reese's® Chewy Chocolate Cookies

2 cups all-purpose flour
¾ cup HERSHEY'S Cocoa
1 teaspoon baking soda
½ teaspoon salt
1¼ cups (2½ sticks) butter or margarine, softened
2 cups sugar
2 eggs
2 teaspoons vanilla extract
1⅔ cups (10-ounce package) REESE'S® Peanut Butter Chips

Heat oven to 350°F. Stir together flour, cocoa, baking soda and salt. In large mixer bowl, beat butter and sugar until light and fluffy. Add eggs and vanilla; beat well. Gradually add flour mixture, beating well. Stir in peanut butter chips. Drop by rounded teaspoonfuls onto ungreased cookie sheet. Bake 8 to 9 minutes. (Do not overbake; cookies will be soft. They will puff while baking and flatten while cooling.) Cool slightly; remove from cookie sheet to wire rack. Cool completely.

Makes about 4½ dozen cookies

Pan Recipe: Spread batter in greased 15½×10½×1-inch jelly-roll pan. Bake at 350°F 20 minutes or until set. Cool completely in pan on wire rack; cut into bars. Makes about 4 dozen bars.

Ice Cream Sandwiches: Prepare Chewy Chocolate Cookies as directed; cool. Press small scoop of vanilla ice cream between flat sides of cookies. Wrap and freeze.

High Altitude Directions: Increase flour to 2 cups plus 2 tablespoons. Decrease baking soda to ¾ teaspoon. Decrease sugar to 1⅔ cups. Add 2 teaspoons water with flour mixture. Bake at 350°F 7 to 8 minutes. Makes about 6 dozen cookies.

Mocha Cookies

2 tablespoons plus 1½ teaspoons instant coffee granules
1½ tablespoons skim milk
⅓ cup packed light brown sugar
¼ cup granulated sugar
¼ cup margarine
1 egg
½ teaspoon almond extract
2 cups all-purpose flour, sifted
¼ cup wheat flakes
½ teaspoon ground cinnamon
¼ teaspoon baking powder

Preheat oven to 350°F. Spray cookie sheets with nonstick cooking spray. Dissolve coffee granules in milk. In large bowl, beat sugars and margarine until smooth and creamy. Beat in egg, almond extract and coffee mixture. Combine flour, wheat flakes, cinnamon and baking powder; gradually beat flour mixture into sugar mixture. Drop by teaspoonfuls onto prepared cookie sheets; flatten with back of fork. Bake 8 to 10 minutes.

Makes about 40 cookies

Favorite recipe from **The Sugar Association, Inc.**

Mocha Cookies

Cowboy Cookies

½ cup butter, softened
½ cup packed light brown sugar
¼ cup granulated sugar
1 egg
1 teaspoon vanilla
1 cup all-purpose flour
2 tablespoons unsweetened cocoa powder
½ teaspoon baking powder
¼ teaspoon baking soda
1 cup uncooked old-fashioned or quick
    cooking oats
1 cup (6 ounces) semisweet chocolate chips
½ cup raisins
½ cup chopped nuts

Preheat oven to 375°F. Lightly grease cookie sheets or line with parchment paper.

Beat butter with sugars in large bowl until blended. Add egg and vanilla; beat until fluffy. Combine flour, cocoa, baking powder and baking soda in small bowl; stir into butter mixture. Add oats, chocolate chips, raisins and nuts. Drop by rounded teaspoonfuls 2 inches apart onto prepared cookie sheets.

Bake 10 to 12 minutes or until lightly browned around edges. Remove to wire racks to cool.

Makes about 4 dozen cookies

Date-Oatmeal Cookies

1 cup all-purpose flour
1 cup DOLE® Chopped Dates or Pitted
    Prunes, chopped
¾ cup quick-cooking oats
1 teaspoon ground cinnamon
¾ teaspoon baking powder
⅔ cup packed brown sugar
1 medium ripe DOLE® Banana, mashed
    (½ cup)
¼ cup margarine, softened
1 egg
1 teaspoon vanilla extract
Vegetable cooking spray

• Combine flour, dates, oats, cinnamon and baking powder in bowl; set aside.

• Beat together sugar, banana, margarine, egg and vanilla until well blended. Add flour mixture; stir until ingredients are moistened.

• Drop dough by rounded teaspoonfuls, 2 inches apart, onto baking sheets sprayed with vegetable cooking spray.

• Bake at 375°F 10 to 12 minutes or until lightly browned. Remove cookies to wire rack; cool. Store in air-tight container.

Makes about 3 dozen cookies

Prep time: 15 minutes
Bake time: 12 minutes

Double Chocolate Walnut Drops

¾ cup (1½ sticks) butter or margarine, softened
¾ cup granulated sugar
¾ cup firmly packed light brown sugar
1 large egg
1 teaspoon vanilla extract
2¼ cups all-purpose flour
⅓ cup unsweetened cocoa powder
1 teaspoon baking soda
½ teaspoon salt
1¾ cups "M&M's"® Chocolate Mini Baking Bits
1 cup coarsely chopped English or black walnuts

Preheat oven to 350°F. Lightly grease cookie sheets; set aside. In large bowl cream butter and sugars until light and fluffy; beat in egg and vanilla. In medium bowl combine flour, cocoa powder, baking soda and salt; add to creamed mixture. Stir in "M&M's"® Chocolate Mini Baking Bits and nuts. Drop by heaping tablespoonfuls about 2 inches apart onto prepared cookie sheets. Bake 12 to 14 minutes for chewy cookies or 14 to 16 minutes for crispy cookies. Cool completely on wire racks. Store in tightly covered container.

Makes about 4 dozen cookies

Variation: Shape dough into 2-inch-thick roll. Cover with plastic wrap; refrigerate. When ready to bake, slice dough into ¼-inch-thick slices and bake as directed.

Loaded Oatmeal Cookies

¾ cup butter or margarine, softened
1 cup packed brown sugar
1 egg
1 tablespoon milk
1 teaspoon vanilla extract
1½ cups uncooked quick oats
1 cup all-purpose flour
½ teaspoon baking soda
½ teaspoon salt
½ teaspoon ground cinnamon
1 cup (6 ounces) semisweet chocolate chips
1 cup (6 ounces) butterscotch chips
¾ cup raisins
½ cup chopped walnuts

Preheat oven to 350°F. Beat butter and brown sugar in large bowl until creamy. Beat in egg, milk and vanilla until light and fluffy. Mix in oats, flour, baking soda, salt and cinnamon until well blended. Stir in chips, raisins and walnuts. Drop rounded tablespoonfuls of dough 2 inches apart onto ungreased cookie sheets.

Bake 12 to 15 minutes or until lightly browned around edges. Cool 2 minutes on cookie sheets. Remove to wire racks; cool completely.

Makes about 3 dozen cookies

Double Chocolate Walnut Drops

Chock-full
O' Chippers

Chocolate Chip 'n Oatmeal Cookies

1 package (18.25 or 18.5 ounces) yellow cake mix
1 cup quick-cooking rolled oats, uncooked
¾ cup butter or margarine, softened
2 eggs
1 cup HERSHEY'S Semi-Sweet Chocolate Chips

Heat oven to 350°F. Beat cake mix, oats, butter and eggs in large bowl. Stir in chocolate chips. Drop by rounded teaspoonfuls onto ungreased cookie sheets.

Bake 10 to 12 minutes or until very lightly browned. Cool slightly; remove from cookie sheets to wire racks. Cool completely.

Makes about 4 dozen cookies

Banana Chocolate Chip Cookies

2 extra-ripe, medium DOLE® Bananas, peeled
1 package (17.5 ounces) chocolate chip cookie mix
½ teaspoon ground cinnamon
1 egg, lightly beaten
1 teaspoon vanilla extract
1 cup toasted wheat germ

• Mash bananas with fork. Measure 1 cup.

• Combine cookie mix and cinnamon. Stir in contents of enclosed flavoring packet, mashed bananas, egg and vanilla until well blended. Stir in wheat germ.

• Drop batter by heaping tablespoonfuls 2 inches apart onto cookie sheets coated with cooking spray. Shape dough into circles with back of spoon. Bake in 375°F oven 10 to 12 minutes or until lightly browned. Cool on wire racks.

Makes 18 cookies

Chocolate Chip 'n Oatmeal Cookies

Sour Cream Chocolate Chip Cookies

1 Butter Flavor* CRISCO® Stick or 1 cup Butter Flavor* CRISCO® all-vegetable shortening
1 cup firmly packed brown sugar
½ cup granulated sugar
½ cup dairy sour cream
¼ cup warm honey
1 egg
2 teaspoons vanilla
2½ cups all-purpose flour
1½ teaspoons baking powder
½ teaspoon salt
2 cups semi-sweet or milk chocolate chips
1 cup coarsely chopped walnuts

*Butter Flavor Crisco is artificially flavored.

1. Heat oven to 375°F. Grease cookie sheet with shortening. Place sheets of foil on countertop for cooling cookies.

2. Combine shortening, brown sugar and granulated sugar in large bowl. Beat at medium speed of electric mixer until well blended. Beat in sour cream, honey, egg and vanilla. Beat until just blended.

3. Combine flour, baking powder and salt. Mix into creamed mixture at low speed until just blended. Stir in chocolate chips and nuts.

4. Drop slightly rounded measuring tablespoonfuls of dough 2 inches apart onto prepared sheet.

5. Bake 10 to 12 minutes or until set. *Do not overbake.* Cool 2 minutes on baking sheet. Remove to foil to cool completely.

Makes about 5 dozen cookies

Double Chocolate Mint Chip Cookies

1½ cups (10-ounce package) NESTLÉ® TOLL HOUSE® Mint Flavored Semi-Sweet Chocolate Morsels, divided
1¼ cups all-purpose flour
¾ teaspoon baking soda
½ teaspoon salt
½ cup butter, softened
½ cup firmly packed brown sugar
¼ cup sugar
½ teaspoon vanilla extract
1 egg
½ cup chopped nuts

MELT over hot (not boiling) water, ¾ cup morsels; stir until smooth. Remove from heat; cool to room temperature.

COMBINE flour, baking soda and salt. Beat butter, brown sugar, sugar and vanilla extract in large mixer bowl. Add melted morsels and egg; beat well. Gradually add flour mixture to butter mixture. Stir in remaining ¾ cup morsels and nuts. Drop by rounded tablespoons onto ungreased baking sheets. Bake in preheated 375°F. oven for 8 to 9 minutes. Cool on baking sheets for 2 to 3 minutes; remove to wire racks to cool completely.

Makes about 1½ dozen (2-inch) cookies

Sour Cream Chocolate Chip Cookies

Dreamy Chocolate Chip Cookies

1¼ cups firmly packed brown sugar
¾ Butter Flavor* CRISCO® Stick or ¾ cup Butter Flavor* CRISCO® all-vegetable shortening
3 eggs, lightly beaten
2 teaspoons vanilla
1 (4-ounce) package German sweet chocolate, melted, cooled
3 cups all-purpose flour
1 teaspoon baking soda
½ teaspoon salt
1 (11½-ounce) package milk chocolate chips
1 (10-ounce) package premium semisweet chocolate pieces
1 cup coarsely chopped macadamia nuts

*Butter Flavor Crisco is artificially flavored.

1. Heat oven to 375°F. Place sheets of foil on countertop for cooling cookies.

2. Combine brown sugar, shortening, eggs and vanilla in large bowl. Beat at low speed of electric mixer until blended. Increase speed to high. Beat 2 minutes. Add melted chocolate. Mix well.

3. Combine flour, baking soda and salt. Add gradually to shortening mixture at low speed.

4. Stir in chocolate chips, chocolate pieces and nuts with spoon. Drop by rounded tablespoonfuls 3 inches apart onto ungreased baking sheets.

5. Bake for 9 to 11 minutes or until set. *Do not overbake.* Cool 2 minutes on baking sheet. Remove cookies to foil to cool completely.
Makes about 3 dozen cookies

Butterscotch Granola Cookies

1½ cups all-purpose flour
1 teaspoon cinnamon
½ teaspoon salt
½ teaspoon baking powder
½ teaspoon baking soda
½ cup butter, softened
½ cup honey
½ cup firmly packed brown sugar
1 egg
1 teaspoon vanilla extract
¼ cup milk
2 cups (12-ounce package) NESTLÉ® TOLL HOUSE® Butterscotch Flavored Morsels
1 cup quick oats, uncooked
1 cup chopped walnuts
¾ cup raisins
¼ cup wheat germ

COMBINE flour, cinnamon, salt, baking powder and baking soda in small bowl. Beat butter, honey and brown sugar in large mixer bowl. Beat in egg and vanilla extract. Add flour mixture alternately with milk to butter mixture. Stir in morsels, oats, walnuts, raisins and wheat germ. Drop by rounded tablespoons onto greased baking sheets.

BAKE in preheated 350°F. oven for 8 to 10 minutes. Cool on baking sheets for 2 minutes; remove to wire racks to cool completely.
Makes about 5 dozen (2¼-inch) cookies

Dreamy Chocolate Chip Cookies

Hershey's Vanilla Chip Chocolate Cookies

1 cup (2 sticks) butter or margarine,
   softened
2 cups sugar
2 eggs
2 teaspoons vanilla extract
2 cups all-purpose flour
¾ cup HERSHEY'S Cocoa
1 teaspoon baking soda
½ teaspoon salt
1⅔ cups (10-ounce package) HERSHEY'S
   Premier White Chips

Heat oven to 350°F. Beat butter and sugar in large bowl until creamy. Add eggs and vanilla; beat until light and fluffy.

Stir together flour, cocoa, baking soda and salt; gradually blend into butter mixture. Stir in white chips. Drop by rounded teaspoons onto ungreased cookie sheets.

Bake 8 to 9 minutes. (*Do not overbake; cookies will be soft. They will puff while baking and flatten upon cooling.*) Cool slightly. Remove from cookie sheets to wire racks; cool completely.
Makes about 4½ dozen cookies

Almond Double Chip Cookies

¾ cup butter or margarine, softened
¾ cup packed light brown sugar
1 egg
½ teaspoon almond extract
1½ cups all-purpose flour
¼ teaspoon baking soda
   Dash salt
1 cup (6 ounces) semisweet chocolate chips
1 cup (6 ounces) vanilla milk chips
½ cup slivered blanched almonds

Preheat oven to 375°F. Line cookie sheets with parchment paper or leave ungreased.

Beat butter and brown sugar in large bowl with electric mixer until creamy. Beat in egg and almond extract.

Combine flour, baking soda and salt in small bowl; blend into butter mixture. Stir in semisweet and vanilla milk chips and almonds. Drop by rounded tablespoonfuls, 3 inches apart, onto prepared cookie sheets. Bake 8 to 10 minutes or until lightly browned. *Do not overbake.* Cool 2 minutes on cookie sheets; remove to wire racks to cool completely.
Makes about 3 dozen cookies

Hershey's Vanilla Chip Chocolate Cookies

Chocolate Chip Caramel Nut Cookies

18 caramels, unwrapped
1 cup Butter Flavor* CRISCO® all-vegetable shortening
1 cup granulated sugar
½ cup firmly packed brown sugar
2 eggs, beaten
2¾ cups all-purpose flour
1 teaspoon baking soda
1 teaspoon salt
1 teaspoon vanilla
½ teaspoon hot water
1 cup HERSHEY'S MINI CHIPS™ Semi-Sweet Chocolate
½ cup coarsely chopped unsalted peanuts

*Butter Flavor Crisco is artificially flavored.

1. Preheat oven to 400°F.

2. Cut each caramel into 4 pieces. Cut each piece into 6 pieces.

3. Combine shortening, granulated sugar and brown sugar in large bowl. Beat at medium speed of electric mixer until well blended and creamy. Beat in eggs.

4. Combine flour, baking soda and salt. Add gradually to shortening mixture at low speed of electric mixer. Mix until well blended. Beat in vanilla and hot water. Stir in caramels, small chocolate chips and nuts with spoon. Drop two slightly rounded tablespoonfuls 3 inches apart on ungreased cookie sheets for each cookie. Shape dough into circles, 2 inches in diameter and 1 inch high.

5. Bake for 7 to 9 minutes or until light golden brown. Cool 5 minutes on cookie sheets before removing to wire racks.

Makes 2 to 2½ dozen cookies

Chunky Chocolate Cookies

1 cup butter, softened
¾ cup granulated sugar
¾ cup packed light brown sugar
2 eggs
1½ teaspoons vanilla
2¼ cups all-purpose flour
1 teaspoon baking soda
½ teaspoon salt
1 cup coarsely chopped walnuts
1 (8-ounce) milk chocolate candy bar, cut into ½-inch pieces

Preheat oven to 375°F. Beat butter, granulated sugar, brown sugar, eggs and vanilla in large bowl until fluffy. Add flour, baking soda and salt. Continue beating until well mixed, 1 to 2 minutes. Stir in walnuts and chocolate. Drop rounded tablespoonfuls of dough 2 inches apart onto ungreased cookie sheets.

Bake 9 to 11 minutes or until lightly browned. Cool 1 minute on cookie sheets. Cool completely on wire racks. *Makes about 3 dozen cookies*

Chunky Chocolate Cookies

Chocolate-Orange Chip Cookies

1¼ cups packed brown sugar
½ Butter Flavor* CRISCO® Stick or ½ cup
    Butter Flavor* CRISCO®
    all-vegetable shortening
2 squares (1 ounce each) unsweetened
    chocolate, melted and cooled
1 egg
2 tablespoons orange juice concentrate
1 teaspoon grated orange peel
1 teaspoon vanilla
1½ cups all-purpose flour
¾ teaspoon baking soda
¼ teaspoon salt
1 cup semisweet chocolate chips
½ cup blanched slivered almonds

*Butter Flavor Crisco is artificially flavored.

1. Heat oven to 375°F. Place sheets of foil on countertop for cooling cookies.

2. Combine brown sugar, shortening and melted chocolate in large bowl. Beat at medium speed of electric mixer until well blended. Beat in egg, orange juice, orange peel and vanilla.

3. Combine flour, baking soda and salt. Mix into shortening mixture at low speed until well blended. Stir in chocolate chips and nuts.

4. Drop tablespoonfuls of dough 2 inches apart onto ungreased baking sheets.

5. Bake one baking sheet at a time at 375°F for 7 to 9 minutes or until set. *Do not overbake*. Cool 2 minutes on baking sheets. Remove cookies to foil to cool completely.

Makes about 3½ dozen cookies

Hershey's More Chips Chocolate Chip Cookies

1½ cups butter, softened
1 cup granulated sugar
1 cup packed light brown sugar
3 eggs
2 teaspoons vanilla extract
3⅓ cups all-purpose flour
1½ teaspoons baking soda
¾ teaspoon salt
4 cups (24-ounce package) HERSHEY'S
    Semi-Sweet Chocolate Chips

Heat oven to 375°F. Beat butter, granulated sugar and brown sugar in large bowl until creamy. Add eggs and vanilla; beat until light and fluffy.

Stir together flour, baking soda and salt; gradually beat into butter mixture. Stir in chocolate chips. Drop by rounded teaspoons onto ungreased cookie sheets.

Bake 8 to 10 minutes or until lightly browned. Cool slightly. Remove from cookie sheets to wire racks; cool completely.

Makes about 7½ dozen cookies

Left to right: Chocolate-Orange Chip Cookies and Cinnamon-Apricot Tart Oatmeal Cookies (page 14)

Ultimate Chocolate Chip Cookies

¾ **Butter Flavor* CRISCO® Stick or** ¾ **cup Butter Flavor* CRISCO® all-vegetable shortening**
1¼ **cups firmly packed brown sugar**
2 **tablespoons milk**
1 **tablespoon vanilla**
1 **egg**
1¾ **cups all-purpose flour**
1 **teaspoon salt**
¾ **teaspoon baking soda**
1 **cup semisweet chocolate chips**
1 **cup coarsely chopped pecans****
  Drizzle (recipe follows, optional)

*Butter Flavor Crisco is artificially flavored.

**You may substitute an additional ½ cup semisweet chocolate chips for pecans.

1. Heat oven to 375°F. Place foil on countertops for cooling cookies.

2. Combine shortening, sugar, milk and vanilla in large bowl. Beat at medium speed of electric mixer until well blended. Beat in egg.

3. Combine flour, salt and baking soda. Mix into shortening mixture at low speed just until blended. Stir in chocolate chips and nuts.

4. Drop by rounded tablespoonfuls 3 inches apart onto ungreased baking sheets.

5. Bake for 8 to 10 minutes for chewy cookies or 11 to 13 minutes for crisp cookies. *Do not overbake.* Cool 2 minutes on baking sheets. Remove to foil to cool completely.

Makes about 3 dozen cookies

Drizzle: Combine 1 teaspoon Butter Flavor* CRISCO® stick and 1 cup semisweet chocolate chips *or* 1 cup white melting chocolate, cut into small pieces, in microwave-safe measuring cup. Microwave at 50% (MEDIUM). Stir after 1 minute. Repeat until smooth. Or melt on rangetop in small saucepan on very low heat. For thinner drizzle, add more Butter Flavor* Crisco®. Drizzle back and forth over cookie. Sprinkle with nuts before chocolate hardens, if desired. To quickly harden chocolate, place cookies in refrigerator to set.

Chocolate Dipped Ultimate Chocolate Chip Cookies: Melt chocolate as directed for Drizzle. Dip half of cooled cookie in chocolate. Sprinkle with finely chopped nuts before chocolate hardens, if desired. Place on waxed paper until chocolate is firm. To quickly harden chocolate, place cookies in refrigerator to set.

Double Chocolate Chip Cookies

2 cups all-purpose flour
1 teaspoon baking soda
½ teaspoon salt
4 cups (24-ounce package) HERSHEY'S Semi-Sweet Chocolate Chips, divided
¾ cup (1½ sticks) butter or margarine, softened
¾ cup sugar
2 eggs

Heat oven to 350°F. Stir together flour, baking soda and salt.

Place 2 cups chocolate chips in medium microwave-safe bowl. Microwave at HIGH (100%) 1½ minutes; stir. Microwave at HIGH an additional 30 seconds or until chips are melted and smooth when stirred; cool slightly.

Beat butter and sugar in large bowl until light and fluffy. Add eggs; beat well. Blend in melted chocolate. Gradually add flour mixture to chocolate mixture, beating well. Stir in remaining 2 cups chips. Drop dough by rounded teaspoon onto ungreased cookie sheets.

Bake 8 to 9 minutes. *Do not overbake.* Cookies should be soft. Cool slightly. Remove from cookie sheets to wire racks; cool completely.

Makes about 5 dozen cookies

Oatmeal Chocolate Chip Cookies

1 can (20 ounces) DOLE® Crushed Pineapple
1½ cups brown sugar, packed
1 cup margarine, softened
1 egg
¼ teaspoon almond extract
4 cups rolled oats, uncooked
2 cups flour
1 teaspoon baking powder
1 teaspoon salt
1 teaspoon ground cinnamon
½ teaspoon ground nutmeg
2 cups flaked coconut
1 package (12 ounces) semisweet chocolate chips
¾ cup DOLE® Slivered Almonds, toasted

• Preheat oven to 350°F. Grease cookie sheets. Drain pineapple well, reserving ½ cup liquid.

• In large bowl, beat brown sugar and margarine until light and fluffy. Beat in egg. Beat in pineapple, reserved ½ cup liquid and almond extract.

• In small bowl, combine oats, flour, baking powder, salt, cinnamon and nutmeg. Add to margarine mixture; beat until blended. Stir in coconut, chocolate chips and almonds. Drop by heaping tablespoonfuls onto prepared cookie sheets. Flatten cookies slightly with back of spoon. Bake 20 to 25 minutes or until golden. Cool on wire racks.

Makes about 5 dozen cookies

Top to bottom: Double Chocolate Chip Cookies and Forgotten Chips Cookies (page 54)

Hershey's Great American Chocolate Chip Cookies

1 cup (2 sticks) butter, softened
¾ cup granulated sugar
¾ cup packed light brown sugar
1 teaspoon vanilla extract
2 eggs
2¼ cups all-purpose flour
1 teaspoon baking soda
½ teaspoon salt
2 cups (12-ounce package) HERSHEY'S
  Semi-Sweet Chocolate Chips
1 cup chopped nuts (optional)

Heat oven to 375°F. Beat butter, granulated sugar, brown sugar and vanilla in large mixer bowl until creamy. Add eggs; beat well.

Stir together flour, baking soda and salt; gradually add to butter mixture, beating well. Stir in chocolate chips and nuts, if desired. Drop dough by rounded teaspoons onto ungreased cookie sheet.

Bake 8 to 10 minutes or until lightly browned. Cool slightly. Remove from cookie sheet to wire rack; cool completely.

Makes about 6 dozen cookies

Hershey's Great American Chocolate Chip Pan Cookies: Spread dough into greased 15½×10½×1-inch jelly-roll pan. Bake at 375°F 20 minutes or until lightly browned. Cool completely in pan on wire rack. Cut into bars. Makes about 4 dozen bars.

SKOR® & Chocolate Chip Cookies: Omit 1 cup HERSHEY'S Semi-Sweet Chocolate Chips and nuts; replace with 1 cup finely chopped SKOR® bars. Drop onto cookie sheets and bake as directed.

Great American Ice Cream Sandwiches: Prepare cookies as directed. Place one small scoop slightly softened vanilla ice cream between flat sides of two cookies. Gently press together. Wrap and freeze.

Peanut Butter Jumbos

½ cup butter, softened
1 cup packed brown sugar
1 cup granulated sugar
1½ cups peanut butter
3 eggs
2 teaspoons baking soda
1 teaspoon vanilla
4½ cups uncooked rolled oats
1 cup (6 ounces) semisweet chocolate chips
1 cup candy-coated chocolate pieces

Preheat oven to 350°F. Lightly grease cookie sheets or line with parchment paper. Beat butter, sugars, peanut butter and eggs in large bowl until well blended. Blend in baking soda, vanilla and oats until well mixed. Stir in chocolate chips and candy pieces.

Scoop out about ⅓ cupful of dough for each cookie. Place on prepared cookie sheets, spacing about 4 inches apart. Press each cookie to flatten slightly. Bake 15 to 20 minutes or until firm in center. Remove to wire racks to cool.

Makes about 1½ dozen cookies

Top to bottom: Cocoa Kiss Cookies (page 154) and Hershey's Great American Chocolate Chip Cookies

Quick

AS A WINK COOKIES

Chocolate Crackletops

2 cups all-purpose flour
2 teaspoons baking powder
2 cups granulated sugar
½ cup (1 stick) butter or margarine
4 squares (1 ounce each) unsweetened baking chocolate, chopped
4 large eggs, lightly beaten
2 teaspoons vanilla extract
1¾ cups "M&M's"® Chocolate Mini Baking Bits
Additional granulated sugar

Combine flour and baking powder; set aside. In 2-quart saucepan over medium heat combine 2 cups sugar, butter and chocolate, stirring until butter and chocolate are melted; remove from heat. Gradually stir in eggs and vanilla. Stir in flour mixture until well blended. Chill mixture 1 hour. Stir in "M&M's"® Chocolate Mini Baking Bits; chill mixture an additional 1 hour.

Preheat oven to 350°F. Line cookie sheets with foil. With sugar-dusted hands, roll dough into 1-inch balls; roll balls in additional granulated sugar. Place about 2 inches apart onto prepared cookie sheets. Bake 10 to 12 minutes. *Do not overbake.* Cool completely on wire racks. Store in tightly covered container.

Makes about 5 dozen cookies

Chocolate Crackletops

Elvis Would Have Loved These Peanut Butter Cookies

COOKIES

1¼ cups firmly packed light brown sugar
¾ cup creamy peanut butter
1 cup mashed banana
½ CRISCO® Stick or ½ cup CRISCO® all-vegetable shortening
3 tablespoons milk
1½ teaspoons vanilla
1 egg
2 cups all-purpose flour
¾ teaspoon baking soda
¾ teaspoon salt
1½ cups milk chocolate chunks or semi-sweet chocolate chips
1 cup coarsely chopped pecans

FROSTING

2 tablespoons Butter Flavor* CRISCO® Stick or 2 tablespoons Butter Flavor* CRISCO® all-vegetable shortening
1½ cups miniature marshmallows
¼ cup creamy peanut butter
½ teaspoon vanilla
1¼ cups confectioners' sugar
   Hot water
1 cup peanut butter chips

*Butter Flavor Crisco is artifically flavored.

1. Heat oven to 350°F. Place sheets of foil on countertop for cooling cookies.

2. For Cookies, place brown sugar, peanut butter, banana, shortening, milk and vanilla in large bowl. Beat at medium speed of electric mixer until well blended. Add egg. Beat just until blended.

3. Combine flour, baking soda and salt. Add to shortening mixture. Beat at low speed just until blended. Stir in chocolate chips and pecans.

4. Drop dough by rounded measuring tablespoonfuls 2 inches apart onto ungreased baking sheets.

5. Bake one baking sheet at a time for 11 to 13 minutes or until cookies are light brown around edges. *Do not overbake*. Cool 2 minutes on baking sheet. Remove cookies to foil to cool completely.

6. For Frosting, melt 2 tablespoons shortening in medium saucepan on low heat. Add marshmallows and peanut butter. Heat until melted, stirring constantly until well blended. Remove from heat. Stir in vanilla.

7. Place confectioners' sugar in medium bowl. Add marshmallow mixture and 1 tablespoon of hot water at a time, beating until desired consistency. Frost cookies. Sprinkle with peanut butter chips.   *Makes about 4 dozen cookies*

Elvis Would Have Loved These Peanut Butter Cookies

Whole-Wheat Oatmeal Cookies

1 cup whole-wheat flour
1 teaspoon ground cinnamon
1 teaspoon baking powder
½ teaspoon baking soda
½ teaspoon salt
1 cup packed light brown sugar
¼ cup unsweetened applesauce
2 egg whites
2 tablespoons margarine
1½ teaspoons vanilla
1⅓ cups uncooked old-fashioned or quick oats
½ cup raisins

Preheat oven to 375°F. Lightly spray cookie sheets with nonstick cooking spray. Set aside.

Combine flour, cinnamon, baking powder, baking soda and salt in medium bowl; mix well. Combine brown sugar, applesauce, egg whites, margarine and vanilla in large bowl. Mix until small crumbs form. Add flour mixture; mix well. Blend in oats and raisins.

Drop by rounded teaspoonfuls onto prepared cookie sheets, 2 inches apart. Bake 10 to 12 minutes or until golden brown. Cool on wire racks.   *Makes 3½ dozen cookies*

Macaroon Kiss Cookies

¾ cup sugar
⅓ cup butter or margarine, softened
1 package (3 ounces) cream cheese, softened
1 egg yolk
2 teaspoons almond extract
2 teaspoons orange juice
1¼ cups all-purpose flour
2 teaspoons baking powder
¼ teaspoon salt
1 package (14 ounces) MOUNDS™ Sweetened Coconut Flakes, divided
1 bag (9-ounces) HERSHEY'S KISSES Milk Chocolates (about 54)

In large bowl, beat together sugar, butter and cream cheese. Add egg yolk, almond extract and orange juice; beat well. Stir together flour, baking powder and salt; gradually add to butter mixture. Stir in 3 cups coconut. Cover tightly; refrigerate 1 hour or until firm enough to handle.

Preheat oven to 350°F. Shape dough into 1-inch balls; roll in remaining coconut. Place on ungreased cookie sheets. Bake 10 to 12 minutes or until lightly browned. Meanwhile, remove wrappers from chocolate pieces. Remove cookies from oven; immediately press chocolate piece in center of each cookie. Cool 1 minute. Carefully remove from cookie sheets; cool completely on wire racks.   *Makes about 4½ dozen cookies*

Cherry Dot Cookies

2¼ cups all-purpose flour
  2 teaspoons baking powder
  ½ teaspoon salt
  ¾ cup margarine, softened
  1 cup sugar
  2 eggs
  2 tablespoons skim milk
  1 teaspoon vanilla
  1 cup chopped nuts
  1 cup finely chopped pitted dates
  ⅓ cup finely chopped maraschino cherries
2⅔ cups *KELLOGG'S CORN FLAKES®*
     cereal, crushed to 1⅓ cups
     Vegetable cooking spray
15 maraschino cherries, cut into quarters

1. Preheat oven to 350°F. Stir together flour, baking powder and salt. Set aside.

2. In large mixing bowl, beat margarine and sugar until light and fluffy. Add eggs. Beat well. Stir in milk and vanilla. Add flour mixture. Mix well. Stir in nuts, dates and ⅓ cup cherries.

3. Shape level tablespoons of dough into balls. Roll in *KELLOGG'S CORN FLAKES®* cereal. Place on baking sheets coated with cooking spray. Top each with cherry quarter.

4. Bake about 10 minutes or until lightly browned. *Makes 5 dozen cookies*

Forgotten Chips Cookies

2 egg whites
⅛ teaspoon cream of tartar
⅛ teaspoon salt
⅔ cup sugar
1 teaspoon vanilla extract
1 cup HERSHEY'S Semi-Sweet Chocolate
    Chips or Milk Chocolate Chips

Preheat oven to 375°F. Lightly grease cookie sheets. In small bowl, beat egg whites with cream of tartar and salt until soft peaks form. Gradually add sugar, beating until stiff peaks form. Carefully fold in vanilla extract and chocolate chips. Drop by teaspoonfuls onto prepared cookie sheets. Place cookie sheets in preheated oven; immediately turn off oven and allow cookies to remain in oven six hours or overnight without opening door. Remove cookies from cookie sheets. Store in airtight container in cool, dry place. *Makes about 2½ dozen cookies*

No-Bake Peanutty Cookies

2 cups Roasted Honey Nut SKIPPY®
    Creamy or SUPER CHUNK® Peanut
    Butter
2 cups graham cracker crumbs
1 cup confectioners' sugar
½ cup KARO® Light or Dark Corn Syrup
¼ cup semisweet chocolate chips, melted
    Colored sprinkles (optional)

1. In large bowl, combine peanut butter, graham cracker crumbs, confectioners' sugar and corn syrup. Mix until smooth.

2. Shape into 1-inch balls. Place on waxed paper-lined cookie sheets.

3. Drizzle melted chocolate over balls; roll in colored sprinkles if desired. Store covered in refrigerator.   *Makes about 5 dozen cookies*

Double Almond Butter Cookies

DOUGH

 2 cups butter, softened
 2½ cups powdered sugar, divided
 4 cups all-purpose flour
 2 teaspoons vanilla

FILLING

 ⅔ cup BLUE DIAMOND® Blanched
     Almond Paste
 ¼ cup packed light brown sugar
 ½ cup BLUE DIAMOND® Chopped Natural
     Almonds, toasted
 ¼ teaspoon vanilla

For Dough, beat butter and 1 cup powdered sugar. Gradually beat in flour. Beat in 2 teaspoons vanilla. Chill dough ½ hour.

For Filling, combine almond paste, brown sugar, almonds and ¼ teaspoon vanilla.

Preheat oven to 350°F. Shape Dough around ½ teaspoon Filling mixture to form 1-inch balls. Place on ungreased cookie sheets.

Bake 15 minutes. Cool on wire racks. Roll cookies in remaining 1½ cups powdered sugar or sift over cookies.   *Makes about 8 dozen cookies*

Cherry Cashew Cookies

 1 cup butter or margarine, softened
 ¾ cup granulated sugar
 ¾ cup packed brown sugar
 2 eggs
 1 teaspoon vanilla extract
 2¼ cups all-purpose flour
 1 teaspoon baking soda
 1 package (10 ounces) vanilla milk chips
     (about 1⅔ cups)
 1½ cups dried tart cherries
 1 cup broken, salted cashews

Preheat oven to 375°F.

Beat butter, granulated sugar, brown sugar, eggs and vanilla in large bowl until fluffy. Combine flour and baking soda in medium bowl; gradually add flour mixture to butter mixture. Stir in vanilla milk chips, dried cherries and cashews. Drop by rounded tablespoonfuls onto ungreased baking sheets.

Bake 12 to 15 minutes or until light golden brown. Cool on wire racks and store in airtight container.   *Makes 4½ dozen cookies*

Favorite recipe from **Cherry Marketing Institute, Inc.**

Chocolate Banana Walnut Drops

½ cup (1 stick) butter or margarine, softened
½ cup solid vegetable shortening
1¼ cups firmly packed light brown sugar
1 large egg
1 medium banana, mashed (about ½ cup)
2¼ cups all-purpose flour
1 teaspoon baking soda
1 teaspoon ground cinnamon
½ teaspoon ground nutmeg
¼ teaspoon salt
2 cups quick-cooking or old-fashioned oats, uncooked
1 cup coarsely chopped walnuts
1¾ cups "M&M's"® Chocolate Mini Baking Bits

Preheat oven to 350°F. In large bowl cream butter, shortening and sugar until light and fluffy; beat in egg and banana. In medium bowl combine flour, baking soda, cinnamon, nutmeg and salt; blend into creamed mixture. Blend in oats and nuts. Stir in "M&M's"® Chocolate Mini Baking Bits. Drop by tablespoonfuls about 2 inches apart onto ungreased cookie sheets. Bake 8 to 10 minutes just until set. *Do not overbake.* Cool 1 minute on cookie sheets; cool completely on wire racks. Store in tightly covered container.   *Makes about 3 dozen cookies*

Cream Cheese Cookies

½ Butter Flavor* CRISCO® Stick or ½ cup Butter Flavor* CRISCO® all-vegetable shortening
1 package (3 ounces) cream cheese, softened
1 tablespoon milk
1 cup sugar
½ teaspoon vanilla
1 cup all-purpose flour
½ cup chopped pecans

*Butter Flavor Crisco is artificially flavored.

1. Heat oven to 375°F. Place sheets of foil on countertop for cooling cookies.

2. Combine shortening, cream cheese and milk in medium bowl at medium speed of electric mixer until well blended. Beat in sugar and vanilla. Mix in flour. Stir in nuts.

3. Drop level measuring tablespoonfuls of dough 2 inches apart onto ungreased baking sheets.

4. Bake one baking sheet at a time for 10 minutes. *Do not overbake.* Cool 2 minutes on baking sheets. Remove cookies to foil to cool completely.   *Makes about 3 dozen cookies*

Lemon or orange variation: Add ½ teaspoon grated lemon or orange peel to dough. Proceed as above.

Chocolate Banana Walnut Drops

Orange Drop Cookies

COOKIES

1 package DUNCAN HINES® Golden
   Sugar Cookie Mix
1 egg
1 tablespoon orange juice
½ teaspoon grated orange peel
¾ cup flaked coconut
½ cup chopped pecans

GLAZE

1 cup confectioners' sugar
2 teaspoons lemon juice
2 teaspoons orange juice
1 teaspoon grated orange peel

1. Preheat oven to 375°F.

2. For Cookies, combine Cookie Mix, buttery flavor packet from Mix, egg, 1 tablespoon orange juice and ½ teaspoon orange peel in large bowl. Stir with spoon until well blended. Stir in coconut and pecans. Drop by rounded teaspoonfuls 2 inches apart onto ungreased cookie sheets. Bake for 7 to 8 minutes or until set. Cool 1 minute on cookie sheets. Remove to cooling racks. Cool completely.

3. For glaze, combine confectioners' sugar, lemon juice, 2 teaspoons orange juice and 1 teaspoon orange peel in small bowl. Stir until blended. Drizzle over top of cooled cookies. Allow glaze to set before storing between layers of waxed paper in airtight container.

Makes about 3 dozen cookies

Chocolate Orange Granola Cookies

1 cup all-purpose flour
½ teaspoon baking powder
½ teaspoon allspice
½ teaspoon salt
⅔ cup firmly packed brown sugar
½ cup butter, softened
1 egg
1 teaspoon vanilla extract
½ teaspoon grated orange peel
1¼ cups granola cereal
1 cup (6-ounce package) NESTLÉ® TOLL
   HOUSE® Semi-Sweet Chocolate
   Morsels
½ cup flaked coconut
¼ cup chopped nuts

COMBINE flour, baking powder, allspice and salt in small bowl. **BEAT** brown sugar and butter in large mixer bowl. Add egg, vanilla extract and orange peel; beat well. Gradually beat in flour mixture. Stir in granola cereal, morsels, coconut and nuts. Drop by rounded tablespoons onto ungreased baking sheets. Sprinkle with additional coconut, if desired.

BAKE in preheated 350°F. oven for 9 to 11 minutes. Cool on baking sheets for 2 minutes; remove to wire racks to cool completely.

Makes about 1½ dozen (2-inch) cookies

Orange Drop Cookies

Blockbuster BROWNIES

Quick & Easy Fudgey Brownies

4 bars (1 ounce each) HERSHEY'S
    Unsweetened Baking Chocolate, broken
    into pieces
¾ cup (1½ sticks) butter or margarine
2 cups sugar
3 eggs
1½ teaspoons vanilla extract
1 cup all-purpose flour
1 cup chopped nuts (optional)
    Quick & Easy Chocolate Frosting
    (recipe follows, optional)

Heat oven to 350°F. Grease 13×9×2-inch baking pan. Place chocolate and butter in large microwave-safe bowl. Microwave at HIGH 1½ to 2 minutes or until chocolate is melted and mixture is smooth when stirred. Add sugar; stir with spoon until well blended. Add eggs and vanilla; mix well. Add flour and nuts, if desired; stir until well blended. Spread into prepared pan.

Bake 30 to 35 minutes or until wooden pick inserted in center comes out almost clean. Cool in pan on wire rack. Frost with Quick & Easy Chocolate Frosting, if desired. Cut into squares.
Makes about 24 brownies

Quick & Easy Chocolate Frosting

3 bars (1 ounce each) HERSHEY'S
    Unsweetened Baking Chocolate, broken
    into pieces
1 cup miniature marshmallows
½ cup (1 stick) butter or margarine, softened
⅓ cup milk
2½ cups powdered sugar
½ teaspoon vanilla extract

Melt chocolate in medium saucepan over low heat, stirring constantly. Add marshmallows; stir frequently until melted. (Mixture will be very thick and will pull away from side of pan.) Spoon mixture into small bowl; beat in butter. Add milk gradually, beating until smooth. Add powdered sugar and vanilla; beat to desired consistency.
Makes about 2¼ cups frosting

Quick & Easy Fudgey Brownies

Decadent Blonde Brownies

1½ cups all-purpose flour
1 teaspoon baking powder
½ teaspoon salt
½ cup butter, softened
¾ cup granulated sugar
¾ cup packed light brown sugar
2 eggs
2 teaspoons vanilla
1 package (10 ounces) semisweet chocolate chunks*
1 jar (3½ ounces) macadamia nuts, coarsely chopped, to measure ¾ cup

*If chocolate chunks are not available, cut 10-ounce, thick chocolate candy bar into ½-inch pieces to equal 1½ cups.

Preheat oven to 350°F. Grease 13×9-inch baking pan. Combine flour, baking powder and salt in small bowl.

Beat butter, granulated sugar and brown sugar in large bowl with electric mixer at medium speed until light and fluffy. Beat in eggs and vanilla. Add flour mixture. Beat at low speed until well blended. Stir in chocolate chunks and macadamia nuts with mixing spoon. Spread batter evenly into prepared baking pan.

Bake 25 to 30 minutes or until golden brown. Remove pan to wire rack; cool completely. Cut into 3¼×1½-inch bars.

Makes 2 dozen brownies

Bittersweet Brownies

MAZOLA® NO STICK® Cooking Spray
4 squares (1 ounce each) unsweetened chocolate, melted
1 cup sugar
½ cup HELLMANN'S® or BEST FOODS® Real or Light Mayonnaise
2 eggs
1 teaspoon vanilla
¾ cup flour
½ teaspoon baking powder
¼ teaspoon salt
½ cup chopped walnuts

1. Preheat oven to 350°F. Spray 8×8×2-inch baking pan with cooking spray.

2. In large bowl, stir chocolate, sugar, mayonnaise, eggs and vanilla until smooth. Stir in flour, baking powder and salt until well blended. Stir in walnuts. Spread evenly in prepared pan.

3. Bake 25 to 30 minutes or until wooden pick inserted into center comes out clean. Cool in pan on wire rack. Cut into 2-inch squares.

Makes 16 brownies

Decadent Blonde Brownies

Bamboozlers

1 cup all-purpose flour
¾ cup packed light brown sugar
¼ cup unsweetened cocoa powder
1 whole egg
2 egg whites
5 tablespoons margarine, melted
¼ cup fat-free (skim) milk
¼ cup honey
1 teaspoon vanilla
2 tablespoons semisweet chocolate chips
2 tablespoons coarsely chopped walnuts
Powdered sugar (optional)

1. Preheat oven to 350°F. Grease and flour 8-inch square baking pan; set aside.

2. Combine flour, brown sugar and cocoa in medium bowl. Blend together whole egg, egg whites, margarine, milk, honey and vanilla in medium bowl. Add to flour mixture; mix well. Pour into prepared baking pan; sprinkle with chocolate chips and walnuts.

3. Bake brownies about 30 minutes or until they spring back when lightly touched in center. Cool completely in pan on wire rack. Sprinkle with powdered sugar just before serving.

Makes 12 brownies

Peanutters: Substitute peanut butter chips for chocolate chips and peanuts for walnuts.

Butterscotch Babies: Substitute butterscotch chips for chocolate chips and pecans for walnuts.

Brownie Sundaes: Serve brownies on dessert plates. Top each brownie with a scoop of vanilla nonfat frozen yogurt and 2 tablespoons nonfat chocolate or caramel sauce.

Drizzle Topped Brownies

1¼ cups all-purpose biscuit baking mix
1 cup sugar
½ cup HERSHEY'S Cocoa
½ cup butter or margarine, melted
2 eggs
1 teaspoon vanilla extract
1 cup HERSHEY'S Semi-Sweet Chocolate Chips or MINI CHIPS™
Quick Vanilla Glaze (recipe follows)

Heat oven to 350°F. Grease 8- or 9-inch square baking pan. In medium bowl, combine baking mix, sugar and cocoa; mix with spoon or fork until thoroughly blended. Add butter, eggs and vanilla, mixing well. Stir in chocolate chips. Spread in prepared pan.

Bake 25 to 30 minutes or until wooden pick inserted in center comes out clean. Cool completely. Drizzle Quick Vanilla Glaze over cooled brownies. Cut into squares.

Makes about 20 brownies

Quick Vanilla Glaze: In small bowl combine ½ cup confectioners' sugar, 1 tablespoon water and ¼ teaspoon vanilla extract; blend well.

Bamboozlers

Irish Brownies

4 squares (1 ounce *each*) semisweet baking
chocolate, coarsely chopped
½ cup butter
½ cup sugar
2 eggs
¼ cup Irish cream liqueur
1 cup all-purpose flour
½ teaspoon baking powder
¼ teaspoon salt
Irish Cream Frosting (recipe follows)

Preheat oven to 350°F. Grease 8-inch square
baking pan. Melt chocolate and butter in
medium, heavy saucepan over low heat, stirring
constantly. Stir in sugar. Beat in eggs, 1 at a time,
with wire whisk. Whisk in Irish cream. Combine
flour, baking powder and salt in large bowl; add
to saucepan. Stir until just blended. Spread batter
evenly in prepared pan.

Bake 22 to 25 minutes or until center is set.
Remove pan to wire rack; cool completely before
frosting. Prepare Irish Cream Frosting. Spread
frosting over cooled brownies. Chill at least 1
hour or until frosting is set. Cut into 2-inch
squares.   *Makes about 16 brownies*

Irish Cream Frosting

2 ounces (¼ cup) cream cheese, softened
2 tablespoons butter, softened
2 tablespoons Irish cream liqueur
1½ cups powdered sugar

Beat cream cheese and butter in small bowl with
electric mixer at medium speed until smooth.
Beat in Irish cream. Gradually beat in powdered
sugar until smooth. Makes about ⅔ cup frosting.

Chocolate Chunk Blonde Brownies

½ cup (1 stick) margarine or butter, softened
1 cup firmly packed brown sugar
1 cup granulated sugar
4 eggs
2 teaspoons vanilla
2 cups all-purpose flour
1 teaspoon CALUMET® Baking Powder
¼ teaspoon salt
1 package (8 ounces) BAKER'S®
Semi-Sweet Chocolate, coarsely chopped
1 cup chopped nuts

HEAT oven to 350°F.

BEAT margarine, sugars, eggs and vanilla until
light and fluffy. Mix in flour, baking powder and
salt until well blended. Stir in chocolate and
nuts. Spread in greased 13×9-inch pan.

BAKE for 30 minutes or until toothpick inserted
into center comes out with moist crumbs. Do not
overbake. Cool in pan; cut into squares.
Makes about 24 brownies

Prep Time: 20 minutes

Irish Brownies

Mini Brownie Cups

¼ cup (½ stick) 60% vegetable oil spread
2 egg whites
1 egg
¾ cup sugar
⅔ cup all-purpose flour
⅓ cup HERSHEY'S Cocoa
½ teaspoon baking powder
¼ teaspoon salt
    Mocha Glaze (recipe follows)

Heat oven to 350°F. Line 24 small muffin cups (1¾ inches in diameter) with paper bake cups or spray with vegetable cooking spray. Melt vegetable oil spread in small saucepan over low heat; cool slightly. Beat egg whites and egg in small bowl until foamy; gradually add sugar, beating until slightly thickened and light in color. Stir together flour, cocoa, baking powder and salt; gradually add to egg mixture, beating until blended. Gradually add vegetable oil spread, beating just until blended. Fill muffin cups ⅔ full with batter. Bake 15 to 18 minutes or until wooden pick inserted in center comes out clean. Remove from pan to wire rack. Cool completely. Prepare Mocha Glaze; drizzle over tops of brownie cups. Let stand until glaze is set.

Makes 24 cups

Mocha Glaze

¼ cup powdered sugar
¾ teaspoon HERSHEY'S Cocoa
¼ teaspoon instant coffee granules
2 teaspoons hot water
¼ teaspoon vanilla extract

Stir together powdered sugar and cocoa in small bowl. Dissolve coffee in water; gradually add to sugar mixture, stirring until well blended. Stir in vanilla.

White Chocolate & Almond Brownies

12 ounces white chocolate, broken into pieces
1 cup unsalted butter
3 eggs
¾ cup all-purpose flour
1 teaspoon vanilla
½ cup slivered almonds

Preheat oven to 325°F. Grease and flour 9-inch square baking pan.

Melt chocolate and butter in large, heavy saucepan over low heat, stirring constantly. (White chocolate may separate.) Remove from heat when chocolate is just melted. With electric hand mixer, beat in eggs until mixture is smooth. Beat in flour and vanilla. Spread batter evenly in prepared pan. Sprinkle almonds evenly over top.

Bake 30 to 35 minutes or just until set in center. Cool completely in pan on wire rack. Cut into 2-inch squares. *Makes about 16 brownies*

Orange Cappuccino Brownies

¾ cup butter
2 squares (1 ounce *each*) semisweet chocolate, coarsely chopped
2 squares (1 ounce *each*) unsweetened chocolate, coarsely chopped
1¾ cups sugar
1 tablespoon instant espresso powder or instant coffee granules
3 eggs
¼ cup orange-flavored liqueur
2 teaspoons grated orange peel
1 cup all-purpose flour
1 package (12 ounces) semisweet chocolate chips
2 tablespoons shortening

Preheat oven to 350°F. Grease 13×9-inch baking pan.

Melt butter and chopped chocolates in large, heavy saucepan over low heat, stirring constantly. Stir in sugar and espresso powder. Remove from heat. Cool slightly. Beat in eggs, 1 at a time, with wire whisk. Whisk in liqueur and orange peel. Beat flour into chocolate mixture until just blended. Spread batter evenly in prepared pan.

Bake 25 to 30 minutes or until center is just set. Remove pan to wire rack. Meanwhile, melt chocolate chips and shortening in small, heavy saucepan over low heat, stirring constantly. Immediately spread hot chocolate mixture over warm brownies. Cool completely in pan on wire rack. Cut into 2-inch squares.

Makes about 2 dozen brownies

Walnut Crunch Brownies

BROWNIE LAYER

4 squares BAKER'S® Unsweetened Chocolate
¾ cup (1½ sticks) margarine or butter
2 cups granulated sugar
4 eggs
1 teaspoon vanilla
1 cup all-purpose flour

WALNUT TOPPING

¼ cup (½ stick) margarine or butter
¾ cup firmly packed brown sugar
2 eggs
2 tablespoons all-purpose flour
1 teaspoon vanilla
4 cups chopped walnuts

Preheat oven to 350°F. Microwave unsweetened chocolate and ¾ cup margarine in large microwavable bowl on HIGH 2 minutes or until margarine is melted. Stir until chocolate is completely melted.

Stir granulated sugar into melted chocolate mixture. Mix in 4 eggs and 1 teaspoon vanilla until well blended. Stir in 1 cup flour. Spread in greased 13×9-inch pan.

Microwave ¼ cup margarine and brown sugar in same bowl on HIGH 1 minute or until margarine is melted. Stir in 2 eggs, 2 tablespoons flour and 1 teaspoon vanilla until completely mixed. Stir in walnuts. Spread mixture over brownie batter.

Bake for 45 minutes or until wooden pick inserted into center comes out with fudgy crumbs. *Do not overbake.* Cool in pan; cut into squares.

Makes about 24 brownies

Praline Brownies

BROWNIES

1 package DUNCAN HINES® Milk
    Chocolate Chunk Brownie Mix
2 eggs
1/3 cup water
1/3 cup CRISCO® Oil or CRISCO®
    PURITAN® Canola Oil
3/4 cup chopped pecans

TOPPING

3/4 cup firmly packed brown sugar
3/4 cup chopped pecans
1/4 cup butter or margarine, melted
 2 tablespoons milk
1/2 teaspoon vanilla extract

1. Preheat oven to 350°F. Grease 9-inch square pan.

2. For brownies, combine brownie mix, eggs, water, oil and 3/4 cup pecans in large bowl. Stir with spoon until well blended, about 50 strokes. Spread in prepared pan. Bake at 350°F for 35 to 40 minutes. Remove from oven.

3. For topping, combine brown sugar, 3/4 cup pecans, melted butter, milk and vanilla extract in medium bowl. Stir with spoon until well blended. Spread over hot brownies. Return to oven. Bake for 15 minutes or until topping is set. Cool completely in pan on wire rack. Cut into bars.

Makes about 16 brownies

Divine Double Dark Brownies

1/2 cup KARO® Light or Dark Corn Syrup
1/2 cup (1 stick) MAZOLA® Margarine or
    butter
5 squares (1 ounce each) semisweet
    chocolate
3/4 cup sugar
3 eggs
1 teaspoon vanilla
1 cup all-purpose flour
1 cup chopped walnuts
    Chocolate Glaze (recipe follows)

1. Preheat oven to 350°F. Grease and flour one 9-inch round cake pan.

2. In large saucepan over medium heat, bring corn syrup and margarine to a boil, stirring occasionally; remove from heat. Add chocolate; stir until melted. Add sugar; beat in eggs, one at a time, until blended. Add vanilla, flour and nuts. Pour into prepared pan.

3. Bake 30 minutes or until wooden pick or cake tester inserted in center comes out clean. Cool in pan 10 minutes. Remove; cool completely on wire rack.

4. Prepare glaze; pour over top and spread on side. Let stand 1 hour. *Makes 8 servings*

Chocolate Glaze: In small saucepan over low heat, melt 3 squares (1 ounce each) semisweet chocolate and 1 tablespoon MAZOLA® Margarine or butter, stirring often. Remove from heat. Stir in 2 tablespoons KARO® Light or Dark Corn Syrup and 1 teaspoon milk until smooth.

Best Brownies

½ cup (1 stick) butter or margarine, melted
1 cup sugar
1 teaspoon vanilla
2 eggs
½ cup all-purpose flour
⅓ cup HERSHEY'S Cocoa
¼ teaspoon baking powder
¼ teaspoon salt
½ cup chopped nuts (optional)
  Creamy Brownie Frosting (recipe follows)

Heat oven to 350°F. Grease 9-inch square baking pan. Combine butter, sugar and vanilla in large bowl. Add eggs; beat well with spoon. Stir together flour, cocoa, baking powder and salt; gradually blend into butter mixture. Stir in nuts.

Spread into prepared pan. Bake 20 to 25 minutes or until brownies begin to pull away from side of pan. Cool; frost with Creamy Brownie Frosting. Cut into squares.   *Makes about 16 brownies*

Creamy Brownie Frosting

3 tablespoons butter or margarine, softened
3 tablespoons HERSHEY'S Cocoa
1 tablespoon light corn syrup or honey
½ teaspoon vanilla
1 cup powdered sugar
1 to 2 tablespoons milk

Beat butter, cocoa, corn syrup and vanilla in small bowl. Add powdered sugar and milk; beat to spreading consistency. Makes about 1 cup frosting.

Peanut Butter Chip Brownies

½ cup butter
4 squares (1 ounce *each*) semisweet chocolate
½ cup sugar
2 eggs
1 teaspoon vanilla
½ cup all-purpose flour
1 package (12 ounces) peanut butter chips
1 cup (6 ounces) milk chocolate chips

Preheat oven to 350°F. Grease 8-inch square baking pan. Melt butter and semisweet chocolate in small, heavy saucepan over low heat, stirring just until chocolate melts completely. Remove from heat; cool. Beat sugar and eggs in large bowl until light and fluffy. Blend in vanilla and chocolate mixture. Stir in flour until blended; fold in peanut butter chips. Spread batter evenly in prepared pan.

Bake 25 to 30 minutes or just until firm and dry in center. Remove from oven; sprinkle milk chocolate chips over top. Place pan on wire rack. When chocolate chips have melted, spread over brownies. Refrigerate until chocolate topping is set. Cut into 2-inch squares.

Makes 16 brownies

Peanut Butter Chip Brownies

Double-Decker Confetti Brownies

¾ cup (1½ sticks) butter or margarine,
   softened
1 cup granulated sugar
1 cup firmly packed light brown sugar
3 large eggs
1 teaspoon vanilla extract
2½ cups all-purpose flour, divided
2½ teaspoons baking powder
½ teaspoon salt
⅓ cup unsweetened cocoa powder
1 tablespoon butter or margarine, melted
1 cup "M&M's"® Semi-Sweet Chocolate
   Mini Baking Bits, divided

Preheat oven to 350°F. Lightly grease 13×9×2-inch baking pan; set aside. In large bowl cream butter and sugars until light and fluffy; beat in eggs and vanilla. In medium bowl combine 2¼ cups flour, baking powder and salt; blend into creamed mixture. Divide batter in half. Blend together cocoa powder and melted butter; stir into one half of the dough. Spread cocoa dough evenly into prepared baking pan. Stir remaining ¼ cup flour and ½ cup "M&M's"® Semi-Sweet Chocolate Mini Baking Bits into remaining dough; spread evenly over cocoa dough in pan. Sprinkle with remaining ½ cup "M&M's"® Semi-Sweet Chocolate Mini Baking Bits. Bake 25 to 30 minutes or until edges start to pull away from sides of pan. Cool completely. Cut into squares. Store in tightly covered container.
Makes 24 brownies

All American Heath® Brownies

⅓ cup butter or margarine
1 square (1 ounce) HERSHEY'S
   Unsweetened Baking Chocolate
1 cup sugar
2 eggs
1 teaspoon vanilla
1 cup all-purpose flour
½ teaspoon baking powder
¼ teaspoon salt
1 package (7.5 ounces) original HEATH®
   Bars, coarsely crushed

Preheat oven to 350°F. Grease bottom of 8-inch square baking pan.

In 1½-quart saucepan over low heat, melt butter and chocolate, stirring occasionally. Blend in sugar. Add eggs, 1 at a time, beating after each addition. Blend in vanilla. Stir together flour, baking powder and salt; add to chocolate mixture and blend. Spread batter in prepared pan.

Bake 20 minutes or until brownie starts to pull away from edge of pan. Remove from oven; sprinkle with Heath® Bars. Cover tightly with foil and cool completely on wire rack. Remove foil; cut into squares.   *Makes about 12 brownies*

Double-Decker Confetti Brownies

Caramel-Layered Brownies

4 squares BAKER'S® Unsweetened
  Chocolate
¾ cup (1½ sticks) margarine or butter
2 cups sugar
3 eggs
1 teaspoon vanilla
1 cup all-purpose flour
1 cup BAKER'S® Semi-Sweet Real
  Chocolate Chips
1½ cups chopped nuts, divided
1 (14-ounce) package caramels
⅓ cup evaporated milk

HEAT oven to 350°F.

MICROWAVE chocolate and margarine in large microwavable bowl on HIGH 2 minutes or until margarine is melted. Stir until chocolate is completely melted.

STIR sugar into melted chocolate mixture. Mix in eggs and vanilla until well blended. Stir in flour. Remove 1 cup of batter; set aside. Spread remaining batter into greased 13×9-inch pan. Sprinkle with chips and 1 cup of the nuts.

MICROWAVE caramels and milk in same bowl on HIGH 4 minutes, stirring after 2 minutes. Stir until caramels are completely melted and smooth. Spoon over chips and nuts, spreading to edges of pan. Gently spread reserved batter over caramel mixture. Sprinkle with the remaining ½ cup nuts.

BAKE for 40 minutes or until toothpick inserted into center comes out with fudgy crumbs. Do not overbake. Cool in pan; cut into squares.

Makes about 24 brownies

Butterscotch Brownies

1 cup butterscotch-flavored chips
¼ cup butter or margarine, softened
½ cup packed light brown sugar
2 eggs
½ teaspoon vanilla
1 cup all-purpose flour
½ teaspoon baking powder
¼ teaspoon salt
1 cup semisweet chocolate chips

Preheat oven to 350°F. Grease 9-inch square baking pan. Melt butterscotch chips in small, heavy saucepan over low heat stirring constantly; set aside.

Beat butter and sugar in large bowl until light and fluffy. Beat in eggs, 1 at a time, beating well after each addition. Beat in vanilla and melted butterscotch chips. Combine flour, baking powder and salt in small bowl; add to butter mixture. Beat until well blended. Spread batter evenly in prepared pan.

Bake 20 to 25 minutes or until golden brown and center is set. Remove pan from oven and immediately sprinkle with chocolate chips. Let stand about 4 minutes or until chocolate is melted. Spread chocolate evenly over top. Place pan on wire rack; cool completely. Cut into 2¼-inch squares. *Makes about 16 brownies*

Butterscotch Brownies

Double "Topped" Brownies

BROWNIES
1 package DUNCAN HINES® Double
    Fudge Brownie Mix
2 eggs
⅓ cup water
¼ cup CRISCO® Oil or CRISCO®
    PURITAN® Canola Oil
½ cup flaked coconut
½ cup chopped nuts

FROSTING
3 cups confectioners' sugar
⅓ Butter Flavor* CRISCO® Stick or ⅓ cup
    Butter Flavor* CRISCO® all-vegetable
    shortening
1½ teaspoons vanilla extract
2 to 3 tablespoons milk

TOPPING
3 squares (3 ounces) unsweetened chocolate
1 tablespoon butter or margarine

*Butter Flavor Crisco is artificially flavored.

1. Preheat oven to 350°F. Grease bottom of 13×9-inch pan.

2. For brownies, combine brownie mix, fudge packet from Mix, eggs, water and oil in large bowl. Stir with spoon until well blended, about 50 strokes. Stir in coconut and nuts. Spread in prepared pan. Bake at 350°F for 27 to 30 minutes or until set. Cool completely.

3. For frosting, combine confectioners' sugar, ⅓ cup shortening and vanilla extract. Stir in milk, 1 tablespoon at a time, until frosting is of spreading consistency. Spread over cooled brownies. Refrigerate until frosting is firm, about 30 minutes.

4. For topping, melt chocolate and 1 tablespoon butter in small bowl over hot water; stir until smooth. Drizzle over frosting. Refrigerate until chocolate is firm, about 15 minutes. Cut into squares. *Makes about 48 brownies*

Deep Dish Brownies

¾ cup (1½ sticks) butter or margarine,
    melted
1½ cups sugar
1½ teaspoons vanilla extract
3 eggs
¾ cup all-purpose flour
½ cup HERSHEY'S® Cocoa
½ teaspoon baking powder
½ teaspoon salt

Preheat oven to 350°F. Grease 8-inch square baking pan.

In medium bowl, blend butter, sugar and vanilla. Add eggs; using spoon, beat well. Combine flour, cocoa, baking powder and salt; gradually add to egg mixture, beating until well blended. Spread batter into prepared pan.

Bake 40 to 45 minutes or until brownies begin to pull away from sides of pan. Cool completely in pan on wire rack. Cut into squares.

Makes about 16 brownies

Variation: Stir 1 cup REESE'S® Peanut Butter Chips or HERSHEY'S Semi-Sweet Chocolate Chips into batter. Proceed as above.

Double "Topped" Brownies

Raspberry Fudge Brownies

½ cup butter
3 squares (1 ounce *each*) bittersweet
    chocolate*
2 eggs
1 cup sugar
1 teaspoon vanilla
¾ cup all-purpose flour
¼ teaspoon baking powder
½ cup sliced or slivered almonds
½ cup raspberry preserves
1 cup (6 ounces) milk chocolate chips

*Bittersweet chocolate is available in specialty food stores. One square unsweetened chocolate plus two squares semisweet chocolate may be substituted.

Preheat oven to 350°F. Grease and flour 8-inch square baking pan.

Melt butter and bittersweet chocolate in small, heavy saucepan over low heat. Remove from heat; cool. Beat eggs, sugar and vanilla in large bowl until light. Beat in chocolate mixture. Stir in flour and baking powder until just blended. Spread ¾ of batter in prepared pan; sprinkle almonds over top.

Bake 10 minutes. Remove from oven; spread preserves over almonds. Carefully spoon remaining batter over preserves, smoothing top. Bake 25 to 30 minutes or just until top feels firm.

Remove from oven; sprinkle chocolate chips over top. Let stand a few minutes until chips melt, then spread evenly over brownies. Cool completely in pan on wire rack. When chocolate is set, cut into 2-inch squares.

Makes 16 brownies

One Bowl® Brownies

4 squares BAKER'S® Unsweetened
    Chocolate
¾ cup (1½ sticks) margarine or butter
2 cups sugar
3 eggs
1 teaspoon vanilla
1 cup all-purpose flour
1 cup chopped nuts (optional)

Heat oven to 350°F (325°F for glass baking dish). Line 13×9-inch baking pan with foil extending over edges to form handles. Grease foil.

Microwave chocolate and margarine in large microwavable bowl on HIGH 2 minutes or until margarine is melted. Stir until chocolate is completely melted.

Stir sugar into chocolate until well blended. Mix in eggs and vanilla. Stir in flour and nuts, if desired, until well blended. Spread in prepared pan.

Bake 30 to 35 minutes or until toothpick inserted into center comes out with fudgy crumbs. Do not overbake. Cool in pan. Lift out of pan onto cutting board. Cut into squares.

Makes 24 brownies

Top of Stove Preparation: Melt chocolate and margarine in heavy 3-quart saucepan on very low heat, stirring constantly. Remove from heat. Continue as directed.

Raspberry Fudge Brownies

Triple Chocolate Brownies

3 squares (1 ounce *each*) unsweetened
    chocolate, coarsely chopped
2 squares (1 ounce *each*) semisweet
    chocolate, coarsely chopped
½ cup butter
1 cup all-purpose flour
½ teaspoon salt
¼ teaspoon baking powder
1½ cups sugar
3 eggs
1 teaspoon vanilla
¼ cup sour cream
½ cup milk chocolate chips
    Powdered sugar (optional)

Preheat oven to 350°F. Lightly grease 13×9-inch baking pan.

Place unsweetened chocolate, semisweet chocolate and butter in medium microwavable bowl. Microwave at HIGH 2 minutes or until butter is melted; stir until chocolate is completely melted. Cool to room temperature.

Combine flour, salt and baking powder in small bowl; stir to combine.

Beat sugar, eggs and vanilla in large bowl with electric mixer at medium speed until slightly thickened. Beat in chocolate mixture until well combined. Add flour mixture; beat until blended. Add sour cream; beat until combined. Stir in milk chocolate chips. Spread mixture evenly into prepared pan.

Bake 20 to 25 minutes or until wooden pick inserted into center comes out almost clean. (Do not overbake.) Cool brownies completely in pan on wire rack. Cut into 2-inch squares. Sprinkle powdered sugar over brownies, if desired.

Store tightly covered at room temperature or freeze up to 3 months.   *Makes 2 dozen brownies*

Rich Chocolate Caramel Brownies

1 package (18.25- to 18.5 ounces) devil's
    food or chocolate cake mix
1 cup chopped nuts
½ cup (1 stick) butter or margarine, melted
1 cup undiluted CARNATION® Evaporated
    Milk, *divided*
35 (10 ounces) light caramels, unwrapped
1 cup (6 ounces) NESTLÉ® TOLL
    HOUSE® Semi-Sweet Chocolate
    Morsels

COMBINE cake mix and nuts in large bowl; stir in butter. Stir in ⅔ *cup* evaporated milk (batter will be thick). Spread *half* of batter into greased 13×9-inch baking pan. Bake in preheated 350°F oven for 15 minutes.

COMBINE caramels and *remaining* evaporated milk in small saucepan. Cook over low heat, stirring contantly, for about 10 minutes or until caramels are melted. Sprinkle chocolate morsels over baked layer; drizzle caramel mixture over top. Drop *remaining* batter by heaping teaspoon over caramel mixture. Bake for additional 20 to 25 minutes (top layer will be soft). Cool completely on wire rack.

Makes about 48 brownies

Triple Chocolate Brownies

Ultimate Designer Brownies

¾ cup HERSHEY'S Cocoa
½ teaspoon baking soda
⅔ cup butter or margarine, melted and
    divided
½ cup boiling water
2 cups sugar
2 eggs
1⅓ cups all-purpose flour
1 teaspoon vanilla extract
¼ teaspoon salt
¾ cup (3½-ounce jar) macadamia nuts,
    coarsely chopped
2 cups (12-ounce package) HERSHEY'S
    Semi-Sweet Chocolate Chips, divided
Vanilla Glaze (recipe follows)

Preheat oven to 350°F. Grease 13×9-inch baking pan or two 8-inch square baking pans.

Stir together cocoa and baking soda; blend in ⅓ cup melted butter. Add boiling water; stir until mixture thickens. Stir in sugar, eggs and remaining ⅓ cup melted butter; stir until smooth. Add flour, vanilla and salt; blend well. Stir in nuts and 1½ cups chocolate chips. Pour into prepared pan(s).

Bake 30 to 35 minutes for square pans or 35 to 40 minutes for rectangular pan or until brownie begins to pull away from sides of pan. Cool completely.

Prepare Vanilla Glaze; spread on top of cooled brownie. Cut brownie into triangles. Place remaining ½ cup chips in top of double boiler over hot, not boiling, water; stir until melted. Place melted chips in pastry bag fitted with small writing tip; pipe signature design on each brownie. *Makes about 24 brownies*

Vanilla Glaze

2 tablespoons butter or margarine
1 tablespoon milk
¼ teaspoon brandy extract
¼ teaspoon rum extract
1 cup powdered sugar

Melt butter and milk in small saucepan over low heat. Remove from heat; add brandy and rum extracts. Gradually add powdered sugar, beating with wire whisk until smooth. If glaze is too thick, add additional milk, ½ teaspoon at a time.
Makes about ½ cup glaze

Whimsical
KIDS' TREATS

Happy Cookie Pops

1½ cups granulated sugar
1 cup butter-flavored solid vegetable
    shortening
2 large eggs
1 teaspoon vanilla extract
2¾ cups all-purpose flour
1 teaspoon baking powder
½ teaspoon baking soda
1¾ cups "M&M's"® Chocolate Mini Baking
    Bits, divided
    Additional granulated sugar
2½ dozen flat wooden ice cream sticks
    Prepared frostings
    Tubes of decorator's icing

In large bowl cream 1½ cups sugar and shortening until light and fluffy; beat in eggs and vanilla. In medium bowl combine flour, baking powder and baking soda; blend into creamed mixture. Stir in 1¼ cups "M&M's"® Chocolate Mini Baking Bits. Wrap and refrigerate dough 1 hour.

Preheat oven to 375°F. Roll 1½ tablespoons dough into ball and roll in granulated sugar. Insert ice cream stick into each ball. Place about 2 inches apart onto ungreased cookie sheets; gently flatten, using bottom of small plate. On half the cookies, make a smiling face by placing some of the remaining "M&M's"® Chocolate Mini Baking Bits on the surface; leave other cookies for decorating after baking. Bake all cookies 10 to 12 minutes or until golden. Cool 2 minutes on cookie sheets; cool completely on wire racks. Decorate cookies as desired using frostings, decorator's icing and remaining "M&M's"® Chocolate Mini Baking Bits. Store in single layer in tightly covered container.

Makes 2½ dozen cookies

Variation: For chocolate cookies, combine ⅓ cup unsweetened cocoa powder with flour, baking powder and baking soda; continue as directed.

Happy Cookie Pops

Hot Dog Cookies

¾ **cup butter, softened**
¼ **cup granulated sugar**
¼ **cup packed light brown sugar**
1 **egg yolk**
1⅓ **cups all-purpose flour**
¾ **teaspoon baking powder**
⅛ **teaspoon salt**
  **Shredded coconut, red and green decorator
    gels, frosting and gummy candies**

1. Combine butter, granulated and brown sugars and egg yolk in medium bowl. Add flour, baking powder and salt; mix well. Cover; refrigerate about 4 hours or until firm. Grease cookie sheets.

2. Use ⅓ of dough to make "hot dogs." Refrigerate remaining dough. Mix food colors in small bowl to get reddish-brown color following chart on back of food color box. Add reserved ⅓ of dough. Mix color throughout dough using wooden spoon.

3. Divide colored dough into 6 equal sections. Roll each section into thin log shape. Round edges. Set aside.

4. To make "buns," divide remaining dough into 6 equal sections. Roll sections into thick logs. Make very deep indentation the length of log in centers; smooth edges to create buns.

5. Lift buns with small spatula and dip sides in sesame seeds. Place 3 inches apart on prepared cookie sheets. Place hot dogs inside buns.

6. Freeze 20 minutes. Preheat oven to 350°F. Bake 17 to 20 minutes or until bun edges are light golden brown. Cool completely on cookie sheets.

7. Top hot dogs with green-tinted shredded coconut for "relish," white coconut for "onions," red decorator gel for "ketchup" and yellow-tinted frosting or whipped topping for "mustard."

Makes 6 hot dog cookies

Tip: To pipe gels and frosting onto Hot Dog Cookies, you can use a resealable plastic sandwich bag as a substitute for a pastry bag. Fold the top of the bag down to form a cuff and use a spatula to fill bag half full with gel or frosting. Unfold top of bag and twist down against filling. Snip tiny tip off one corner of bag. Hold top of bag tightly and squeeze filling through opening.

Chocolate Peanut Butter Cookies

1 **package DUNCAN HINES® Moist
    Deluxe Devil's Food Cake Mix**
¾ **cup JIF® Extra Crunchy Peanut Butter**
2 **eggs**
2 **tablespoons milk**
1 **cup candy-coated peanut butter pieces**

1. Preheat oven to 350°F. Grease cookie sheets.

2. Combine cake mix, peanut butter, eggs and milk in large bowl. Mix at low speed with electric mixer until blended. Stir in peanut butter pieces.

3. Drop dough by slightly rounded tablespoonfuls onto prepared cookie sheets. Bake 7 to 9 minutes or until lightly browned. Cool 2 minutes on cookie sheets. Remove to cooling racks.

Makes about 3½ dozen cookies

Hot Dog Cookies

Smushy Cookies

1 package (20 ounces) refrigerated cookie
     dough, any flavor
All-purpose flour (optional)
Peanut butter, multi-colored miniature
     marshmallows, assorted colored
     sprinkles, chocolate-covered raisins and
     caramel candy squares

1. Preheat oven to 350°F. Grease cookie sheets.

2. Remove dough from wrapper according to
package directions.

3. Cut dough into 4 equal sections. Reserve
1 section; refrigerate remaining 3 sections.

4. Roll reserved dough to ¼-inch thickness.
Sprinkle with flour to minimize sticking, if
necessary.

5. Cut out cookies using 2½-inch round cookie
cutter. Transfer to prepared cookie sheets. Repeat
with remaining dough.

6. Bake 8 to 11 minutes or until edges are light
golden brown. Remove to wire racks; cool
completely.

7. To make sandwich, spread about 1½ tablespoons
peanut butter on underside of 1 cookie to within
¼ inch of edge. Sprinkle with miniature
marshmallows and candy pieces.

8. Top with second cookie, pressing gently.
Repeat with remaining cookies and fillings.

9. Just before serving, place sandwiches on paper
towels. Microwave on HIGH (100%) 15 to 25
seconds or until fillings become soft.
     Makes about 8 to 10 sandwich cookies

Tip: Invite the neighbor kids over on a rainy day
to make these fun Smushy Cookies. Be sure to
have lots of filling choices available so each child
can create their own unique cookies.

Butter Pretzel Cookies

¾ cup butter, softened
¼ cup granulated sugar
¼ cup packed light brown sugar
1 egg yolk
1⅓ cups all-purpose flour
¾ teaspoon baking powder
⅛ teaspoon salt
     White, rainbow or colored rock or coarse
     sugar

1. Combine butter, granulated and brown sugars
and egg yolk in medium bowl. Add flour, baking
powder and salt; mix well. Cover; refrigerate
about 4 hours or until firm.

2. Preheat oven to 350°F. Grease cookie sheets.

3. Divide dough into 4 equal sections. Reserve
1 section; refrigerate remaining 3 sections. Divide
reserved dough into 4 equal pieces. Roll each
dough piece on lightly floured surface to 12-inch
rope; sprinkle with rock or coarse sugar.

4. Transfer 1 rope at a time to prepared cookie
sheets. Form each rope into pretzel shape. Repeat
steps with remaining dough pieces.

5. Bake 14 to 18 minutes or until edges begin to
brown. Cool cookies on cookie sheets 1 minute.
Remove to wire racks; cool completely.
     Makes 16 cookies

Smushy Cookies

Domino Cookies

1 package (20 ounces) refrigerated sugar
　　cookie dough
All-purpose flour (optional)
½ cup semisweet chocolate chips

1. Preheat oven to 350°F. Grease cookie sheets.

2. Remove dough from wrapper according to package directions. Cut dough into 4 equal sections. Reserve 1 section; refrigerate remaining 3 sections.

3. Roll reserved dough to ⅛-inch thickness. Sprinkle with flour to minimize sticking, if necessary.

4. Cut out 9 (1¾×2½-inch) rectangles. Place 2 inches apart on prepared cookies sheets.

5. Score each cookie across middle with sharp knife. Gently press chocolate chips, point side down, into dough to resemble various dominos. Repeat with remaining dough and scraps.

6. Bake 8 to 10 minutes or until edges are light golden brown. Remove to wire racks; cool completely.　　　　　　　*Makes 3 dozen cookies*

Tip: Use these adorable cookies as a learning tool for kids. They can count the number of chocolate chips in each cookie and arrange them in lots of ways: highest to lowest, numerically or even solve simple math problems. As a treat, they can eat the cookies afterwards.

Candy Bar Cookies

1 package DUNCAN HINES® Chocolate
　　Chip Cookie Mix
¼ cup unsweetened cocoa powder
1 egg

CARAMEL LAYER

1 package (14 ounces) caramels, unwrapped
⅓ cup evaporated milk
⅓ cup butter or margarine
1⅔ cups confectioners' sugar
1 cup chopped pecans

CHOCOLATE DRIZZLE

½ cup semisweet chocolate chips
2 teaspoons CRISCO® all-vegetable
　　shortening

1. Preheat oven to 375°F.

2. For cookie crust, combine cookie mix and cocoa in large bowl. Stir until blended. Add buttery flavor packet from Mix and egg. Stir until well blended. Press into bottom of ungreased 13×9-inch pan. Bake 14 to 16 minutes or until set.

3. For caramel layer, place caramels, evaporated milk and butter in microwave-safe bowl. Microwave on MEDIUM (50%) for 45 seconds. Stir. Repeat, if necessary, until melted and smooth. Stir in confectioners' sugar until smooth. Stir in pecans. Pour over warm cookie crust.

4. For chocolate drizzle, melt chocolate chips and shortening in small bowl over hot water. Stir until blended. Drizzle over caramel layer. Refrigerate until chocolate is firm. Cut into bars.
　　　　　　　　Makes about 48 bars

Domino Cookies

Ultimate Rocky Road Cups

¾ cup (1½ sticks) butter or margarine
4 squares (1 ounce each) unsweetened
    baking chocolate
1½ cups granulated sugar
3 large eggs
1 cup all-purpose flour
1¾ cups "M&M's"® Chocolate Mini Baking
    Bits
¾ cup coarsely chopped peanuts
1 cup mini marshmallows

Preheat oven to 350°F. Generously grease
24 (2½-inch) muffin cups or line with foil liners.
Place butter and chocolate in large microwave-
safe bowl. Microwave on HIGH 1 minute; stir.
Microwave on HIGH an additional 30 seconds;
stir until chocolate is completely melted. Add
sugar and eggs, one at a time, beating well after
each addition; blend in flour. In separate bowl
combine "M&M's"® Chocolate Mini Baking Bits
and nuts; stir 1 cup baking bits mixture into
brownie batter. Divide batter evenly among
prepared muffin cups. Bake 20 minutes. Combine
remaining baking bits mixture with
marshmallows; divide evenly among muffin cups,
topping hot brownies. Return to oven; bake
5 minutes longer. Cool completely before
removing from muffin cups. Store in tightly
covered container.   *Makes 24 cups*

Mini Ultimate Rocky Road Cups: Prepare
recipe as directed above, dividing batter among
60 generously greased 2-inch mini muffin cups.
Bake 15 minutes. Sprinkle with topping mixture;
bake 5 minutes longer. Cool completely before
removing from cups. Store in tightly covered
container. Makes about 60 mini cups.

Ultimate Rocky Road Squares: Prepare recipe as
directed above, spreading batter into generously
greased 13×9×2-inch baking pan. Bake 30
minutes. Sprinkle with topping mixture; bake
5 minutes longer. Cool completely. Cut into
squares. Store in tightly covered container. Makes
24 squares.

Chocolate-Peanut Cookies

1 cup butter, softened
¾ cup granulated sugar
¾ cup packed light brown sugar
2 eggs
1 teaspoon vanilla
1 teaspoon baking soda
¼ teaspoon salt
2¼ cups all-purpose flour
2 cups chocolate-covered peanuts

Preheat oven to 375°F. Line cookie sheets with
parchment paper or leave ungreased.

Beat butter, sugars, eggs and vanilla in large bowl
until light and fluffy. Mix in baking soda and salt.
Stir in flour to make stiff dough. Stir in
chocolate-covered peanuts. Drop dough by
rounded teaspoonfuls 2 inches apart onto cookie
sheets.

Bake 9 to 11 minutes or until just barely golden.
Do not overbake. Remove to wire racks to cool.
                    Makes about 5 dozen cookies

Ultimate Rocky Road Cups

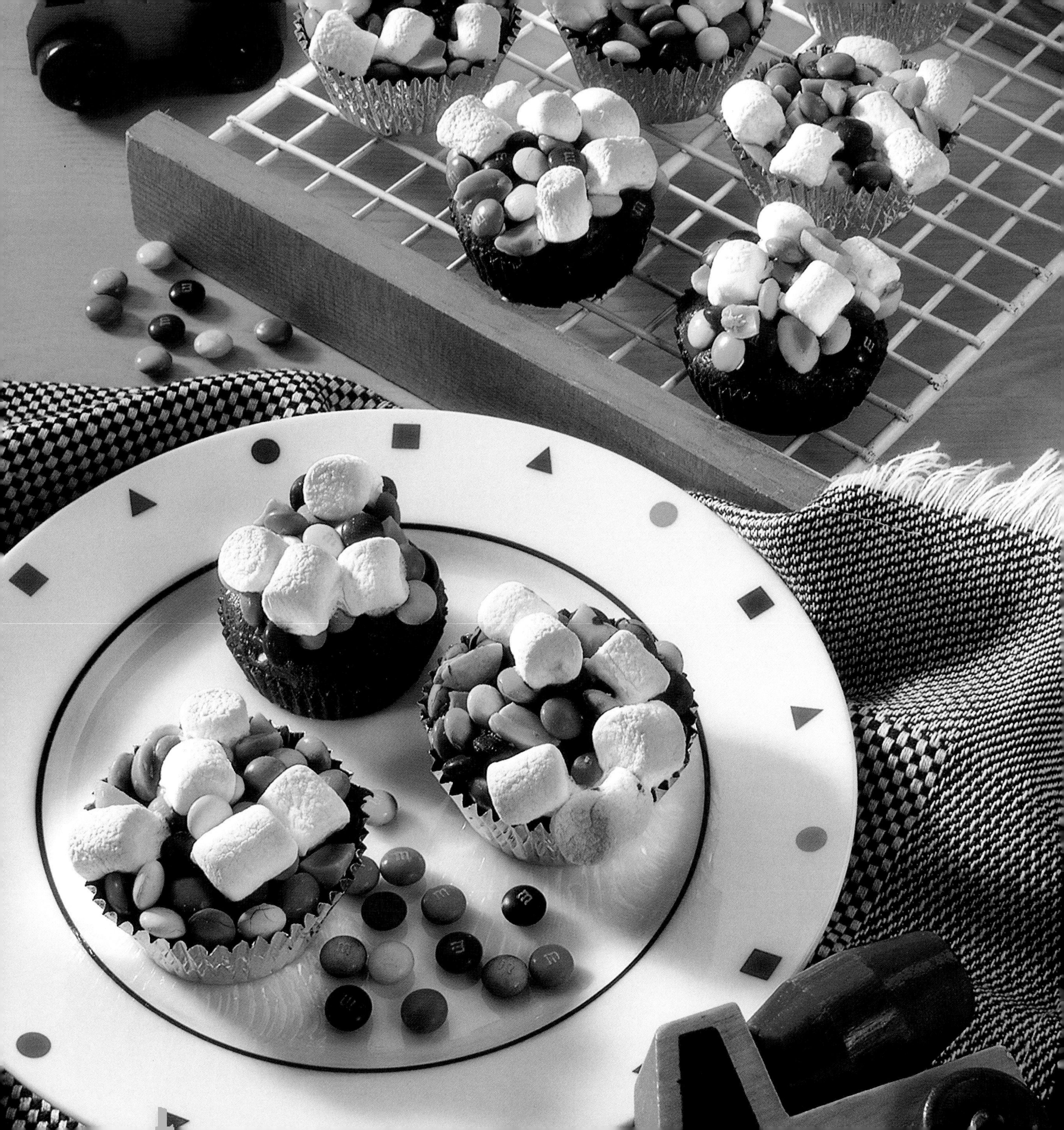

Peanut Butter and Chocolate Cookie Sandwich Cookies

½ cup REESE'S® Peanut Butter Chips
3 tablespoons plus ½ cup butter or margarine, softened and divided
1¼ cups sugar, divided
¼ cup light corn syrup
1 egg
1 teaspoon vanilla extract
2 cups plus 2 tablespoons all-purpose flour, divided
2 teaspoons baking soda
¼ teaspoon salt
½ cup HERSHEY'S Cocoa
5 tablespoons butter or margarine, melted
Sugar
About 2 dozen large marshmallows

Heat oven to 350°F. Melt peanut butter chips and 3 tablespoons softened butter in small saucepan over very low heat. Remove from heat; cool slightly.

Beat remaining ½ cup softened butter and 1 cup sugar in large bowl until light and fluffy. Add corn syrup, egg and vanilla; blend thoroughly. Stir together 2 cups flour, baking soda and salt; add to butter mixture, blending well. Remove 1¼ cups batter and place in small bowl; with wooden spoon stir in the remaining 2 tablespoons flour and peanut butter chip mixture.

Blend cocoa, remaining ¼ cup sugar and 5 tablespoons melted butter into remaining batter. Refrigerate both batters 5 to 10 minutes or until firm enough to handle. Roll each dough into

1-inch balls; roll in sugar. Place on ungreased cookie sheets.

Bake 10 to 11 minutes or until set. Cool slightly; remove from cookie sheets to wire racks. Cool completely. Place 1 marshmallow on flat side of 1 chocolate cookie. Microwave at MEDIUM (50%) 10 seconds or until marshmallow is softened; place a peanut butter cookie over marshmallow, pressing down slightly. Repeat for remaining cookies. Serve immediately.
Makes about 2 dozen cookie sandwiches

Jumbles

½ cup (1 stick) butter or margarine, softened
½ cup granulated sugar
¼ cup firmly packed light brown sugar
1 large egg
1¼ cups all-purpose flour
½ teaspoon baking soda
1¾ cups "M&M's"® Chocolate Mini Baking Bits
1 cup raisins
1 cup chopped walnuts

Preheat oven to 350°F. Lightly grease cookie sheets. Cream butter and sugars until light and fluffy; beat in egg. Combine flour and baking soda; blend into creamed mixture. Stir in remaining ingredients. Drop by rounded tablespoonfuls onto cookie sheets. Bake 13 to 15 minutes. Cool 2 to 3 minutes on cookie sheets; cool completely on wire racks.
Makes about 3 dozen cookies

Peanut Butter and Chocolate Cookie Sandwich Cookies

Brian's Buffalo Cookies

1 Butter Flavor* CRISCO® stick or 1 cup
    Butter Flavor* CRISCO® all-vegetable
    shortening, melted
1 cup granulated sugar
1 cup firmly packed brown sugar
2 tablespoons milk
1 teaspoon vanilla
2 eggs
2 cups all-purpose flour
1 teaspoon baking powder
1 teaspoon baking soda
½ teaspoon salt
1 cup rolled oats (quick or old fashioned),
    uncooked
1 cup corn flakes, crushed to equal ½ cup
1 cup semisweet chocolate chips
½ cup chopped pecans
½ cup flake coconut

*Butter Flavor Crisco is artificially flavored.

1. Preheat oven to 350°F. Grease cookie sheets
with shortening.

2. Combine shortening, granulated sugar, brown
sugar, milk and vanilla in large bowl. Beat at low
speed of electric mixer until well blended. Add
eggs; beat at medium speed until well blended.

3. Combine flour, baking powder, baking soda
and salt. Add gradually to shortening mixture at
low speed. Stir in oats, corn flakes, chocolate
chips, nuts and coconut. Fill ice cream scoop that
holds ¼ cup with dough (or use ¼ cup measuring
cup). Level with knife. Drop 3 inches apart onto
prepared cookie sheets.

4. Bake at 350°F for 13 to 15 minutes or until
lightly browned around edges but still slightly soft
in center. *Do not overbake.* Cool 3 minutes on
cookie sheets before removing to cooling racks
with wide, thin pancake turner.

Makes 2 to 2½ dozen cookies

Cheery Chocolate Animal Cookies

1 (10-ounce) package REESE'S® Peanut
    Butter Chips
1 cup (6 ounces) HERSHEY®S Semi-Sweet
    Chocolate Chips
2 tablespoons shortening (*do not use butter,
    margarine or oil*)
1 (20-ounce) package chocolate sandwich
    cookies
1 (11-ounce) package animal crackers

Line trays or cookie sheets with waxed paper.
Combine chips and shortening in 2-quart glass
measuring cup with handle. Microwave on HIGH
(100% power) 1½ to 2 minutes or until chips are
melted and mixture is smooth when stirred. With
fork, dip each cookie into melted chip mixture;
gently tap fork on side of cup to remove excess
chocolate. Place chocolate coated cookies on
prepared trays; top each cookie with an animal
cracker. Chill until chocolate is set, about 30
minutes. Store in airtight container in a cool, dry
place.   *Makes about 4 dozen cookies*

Cheery Chocolate Animal Cookies

Nutty Sunflower Cookies

1 package (20 ounces) refrigerated peanut
    butter cookie dough
⅓ cup all-purpose flour
½ cup semisweet chocolate chips
½ cup unsalted sunflower seeds
    Yellow and green icing

1. Remove dough from wrapper according to package directions. Combine dough and flour in large bowl; mix well with wooden spoon.

2. Divide dough into 8 equal sections. Preheat oven to 375°F.

3. For each sunflower, divide 1 dough section in half. Roll one half into ball; flatten on ungreased cookie sheet to 2½-inch thickness.

4. Roll other half into 5-inch long rope. Cut 2 inches from rope for stem.

5. Cut remaining 3 inches into 10 equal sections; roll into small balls.

6. Arrange stem and small balls around large ball according to photo on cookie sheet. Repeat with remaining dough.

7. Bake 10 to 11 minutes or until lightly browned. Cool 4 minutes on cookie sheets. Remove to wire racks; cool completely.

8. Melt chocolate chips in microwavable bowl at HIGH (100%) 1½ minutes or until smooth, stirring after 1 minute.

9. Spread melted chocolate in center of each cookie; sprinkle with sunflower seeds.

10. Decorate petals with yellow icing according to photo. Decorate stem with green icing or additional melted chocolate, if desired.

Makes 8 cookies

PB & J Cookie Sandwiches

½ cup butter or margarine, softened
½ cup creamy peanut butter
¼ cup solid vegetable shortening
1 cup firmly packed light brown sugar
1 large egg
1 teaspoon vanilla extract
1⅔ cups all-purpose flour
1 teaspoon baking soda
½ teaspoon baking powder
1 cup "M&M's"® Milk Chocolate Mini
    Baking Bits
½ cup finely chopped peanuts
½ cup grape or strawberry jam

Preheat oven to 350°F. In large bowl cream butter, peanut butter, shortening and sugar until light and fluffy; beat in egg and vanilla. In medium bowl combine flour, baking soda and baking powder; blend into creamed mixture. Stir in "M&M's"® Milk Chocolate Mini Baking Bits and nuts. Drop by rounded teaspoonfuls onto ungreased cookie sheets. Bake 8 to 10 minutes or until light golden. Let cool 2 minutes on cookie sheets; remove to wire racks to cool completely. Just before serving, spread ½ teaspoon jam on bottom of one cookie; top with second cookie. Store in tightly covered container.

Makes about 2 dozen sandwich cookies

Nutty Sunflower Cookies

Peanut Butter Bears

1 cup SKIPPY® Creamy Peanut Butter
1 cup (2 sticks) MAZOLA® Margarine or butter, softened
1 cup packed brown sugar
⅔ cup KARO® Light or Dark Corn Syrup
2 eggs
4 cups all-purpose flour, divided
1 tablespoon baking powder
1 teaspoon cinnamon (optional)
¼ teaspoon salt

1. In large bowl with mixer at medium speed, beat peanut butter, margarine, brown sugar, corn syrup and eggs until smooth. Reduce speed; beat in 2 cups of flour, baking powder, cinnamon and salt. With spoon stir in remaining 2 cups flour. Wrap dough in plastic wrap; refrigerate 2 hours.

2. Preheat oven to 325°F. Divide dough in half; set aside half.

3. On floured surface roll out half of dough to ⅛-inch thickness. Cut with floured bear cookie cutter. Repeat with remaining dough.

4. Bake bears on ungreased cookie sheets 10 minutes or until lightly browned. Remove from cookie sheets; cool completely on wire rack. Decorate as desired.   *Makes about 3 dozen bears*

Tip: Use scraps of dough to make bear faces. Make one small ball of dough for muzzle. Form 3 smaller balls of dough and press gently to create eyes and nose; bake as directed. If desired, use frosting to create paws, ears and bow ties.

Granola Apple Cookies

1 cup packed brown sugar
¾ cup margarine or butter, softened
1 egg
¾ cup MOTT'S® Natural Apple Sauce
1 teaspoon vanilla
3 cups granola with dates and raisins
1½ cups all-purpose flour
1 cup flaked coconut
1 cup unsalted sunflower nuts
1 teaspoon baking powder
1 teaspoon ground cinnamon
½ teaspoon baking soda
½ teaspoon salt
½ teaspoon allspice

In large bowl, combine brown sugar, margarine, egg, apple sauce and vanilla; beat well. Stir in remaining ingredients; mix well. Refrigerate 1 to 2 hours or until firm enough to handle.

Preheat oven to 375°F. Grease cookie sheets. Drop dough by teaspoonfuls 2 inches apart onto prepared cookie sheets. Bake 11 to 13 minutes or until edges are light golden brown. Immediately remove from cookie sheets. Cool on wire racks. Store cookies in airtight container to retain their soft, chewy texture.

Makes about 5 dozen cookies

Tip: For larger cookies, press ¼ cup dough for each cookie 3 inches apart onto greased cookie sheets. Bake at 375°F for 13 to 15 minutes.

Peanut Butter Bears

Marshmallow Sandwich Cookies

⅔ cup butter
1¼ cups sugar
¼ cup light corn syrup
1 egg
1 teaspoon vanilla
2 cups all-purpose flour
½ cup unsweetened cocoa powder
2 teaspoons baking soda
¼ teaspoon salt
   Sugar for rolling
24 large marshmallows

Preheat oven to 350°F. Beat butter and 1¼ cups sugar in large bowl until light and fluffy. Beat in corn syrup, egg and vanilla. Combine flour, cocoa, baking soda and salt in medium bowl; add to butter mixture. Beat until well blended. Cover and refrigerate dough 15 minutes or until firm enough to roll into balls.

Place sugar in shallow dish. Roll tablespoonfuls of dough into 1-inch balls; roll in sugar to coat. Place 3 inches apart on ungreased cookie sheets. Bake 10 to 11 minutes or until set. Remove cookies to wire rack; cool completely.

To assemble sandwiches, place one marshmallow on flat side of one cookie on paper plate. Microwave at HIGH 12 seconds or until marshmallow just begins to melt. Immediately place another cookie, flat side down, on top of hot marshmallow; press together slightly.
Makes about 2 dozen sandwich cookies

Chewy Oatmeal Cookies

¾ Butter Flavor* CRISCO® Stick or ¾ cup Butter Flavor* CRISCO® all-vegetable shortening
1¼ cups firmly packed light brown sugar
1 egg
⅓ cup milk
1½ teaspoons vanilla
3 cups quick cooking oats, uncooked
1 cup all-purpose flour
½ teaspoon baking soda
½ teaspoon salt
¼ teaspoon ground cinnamon
1 cup raisins
1 cup coarsely chopped walnuts

*Butter Flavor Crisco is artificially flavored.

1. Heat oven to 375°F. Grease baking sheets with shortening. Place sheets of foil on countertop for cooling cookies.

2. Combine shortening, brown sugar, egg, milk and vanilla in large bowl. Beat at medium speed of electric mixer until well blended.

3. Combine oats, flour, baking soda, salt and cinnamon. Mix into creamed mixture at low speed just until blended. Stir in raisins and nuts.

4. Drop rounded tablespoonfuls of dough 2 inches apart onto prepared baking sheet.

5. Bake one baking sheet at a time at 375°F for 10 to 12 minutes, or until lightly browned. *Do not overbake*. Cool 2 minutes on baking sheet. Remove cookies to foil to cool completely.
Makes about 2½ dozen cookies

Marshmallow Sandwich Cookies

Brownie Turtle Cookies

2 squares (1 ounce each) unsweetened
    baking chocolate
⅓ cup solid vegetable shortening
1 cup granulated sugar
½ teaspoon vanilla extract
2 large eggs
1¼ cups all-purpose flour
½ teaspoon baking powder
½ teaspoon salt
1 cup "M&M's"® Milk Chocolate Mini
    Baking Bits, divided
1 cup pecan halves
⅓ cup caramel ice cream topping
⅓ cup shredded coconut
⅓ cup finely chopped pecans

Preheat oven to 350°F. Lightly grease cookie
sheets; set aside. Heat chocolate and shortening
in 2-quart saucepan over low heat, stirring
constantly until melted; remove from heat. Mix
in sugar, vanilla and eggs. Blend in flour, baking
powder and salt. Stir in ⅔ cup "M&M's"® Milk
Chocolate Mini Baking Bits. For each cookie,
arrange 3 pecan halves, with ends almost
touching at center, on prepared cookie sheets.
Drop dough by rounded teaspoonfuls onto center
of each group of pecans; mound the dough
slightly. Bake 8 to 10 minutes just until set. *Do
not overbake.* Cool completely on wire racks. In
small bowl combine ice cream topping, coconut
and nuts; top each cookie with about 1½ teaspoons
mixture. Press remaining ⅓ cup "M&M's"® Milk
Chocolate Mini Baking Bits into topping.
Makes about 2½ dozen cookies

Chocolate Malted Cookies

½ cup butter, softened
½ cup shortening
1¾ cups powdered sugar, divided
1 teaspoon vanilla
2 cups all-purpose flour
1 cup malted milk powder, divided
¼ cup unsweetened cocoa powder

1. Beat butter, shortening, ¾ cup powdered sugar
and vanilla in large bowl at high speed of electric
mixer.

2. Add flour, ½ cup malted milk powder and
cocoa; beat at low speed until well blended.
Refrigerate several hours or overnight.

3. Preheat oven to 350°F. Shape slightly
mounded teaspoonfuls of dough into balls. Place
dough balls about 2 inches apart on ungreased
cookie sheets.

4. Bake 14 to 16 minutes or until lightly
browned.

5. Meanwhile, combine remaining 1 cup
powdered sugar and ½ cup malted milk powder in
medium bowl.

6. Remove cookies to wire racks; cool 5 minutes.
Roll cookies in powdered sugar mixture.
Makes about 4 dozen cookies

Tip: Substitute 6 ounces melted semisweet
chocolate for the 1 cup powdered sugar and
½ cup malted milk powder used to roll the
cookies. Instead, dip cookies in melted chocolate
and let dry on wire racks until coating is set.

Brownie Turtle Cookies

Sunshine Butter Cookies

¾ **cup butter, softened**
¾ **cup sugar**
1 **egg**
2¼ **cups all-purpose flour**
¼ **teaspoon salt**
   Grated peel of ½ **lemon**
1 **teaspoon frozen lemonade concentrate,**
   thawed
   Lemonade Royal Icing (recipe follows)
1 **egg, beaten**
   Thin pretzel sticks
   Yellow paste food color
   Gummy fruit and black licorice strings

1. Beat butter and sugar in large bowl at high speed of electric mixer until fluffy. Add egg; beat well.

2. Combine flour, salt and lemon peel in medium bowl. Add to butter mixture. Stir in lemonade concentrate. Refrigerate 2 hours.

3. Prepare Lemonade Royal Icing. Cover; let stand at room temperature. Preheat oven to 350°F. Grease cookie sheets.

4. Roll dough on floured surface to ⅛-inch thickness. Cut out cookies using 3-inch round cookie cutter. Place cookies on prepared cookie sheets. Brush cookies with beaten egg. Arrange pretzel sticks around edge of cookies to resemble sunshine rays; press gently. Bake 10 minutes or until lightly browned. Remove to wire racks; cool completely.

5. Add food color to Lemonade Royal Icing. Spoon about ½ cup icing into resealable plastic food storage bag; seal. Cut tiny tip from corner of bag. Pipe thin circle around underside of each cookie to create outline.

6. Add water, 1 tablespoon at a time, to remaining icing in bowl, until thick but pourable consistency. Spoon icing in cookie centers staying within outline.

7. Decorate cookies with gummy fruit and licorice as shown in photo. Let stand 1 hour or until dry.   *Makes about 3 dozen cookies*

Lemonade Royal Icing

3¾ **cups sifted powdered sugar**
3 **tablespoons meringue powder**
6 **tablespoons frozen lemonade concentrate,**
   thawed

Beat all ingredients in large bowl at high speed of electric mixer until smooth.

Sunshine Butter Cookies

Mom's Best Oatmeal Cookies

¾ **Butter Flavor* CRISCO® Stick or ¾ cup
   Butter Flavor* CRISCO® all-vegetable
   shortening**
1¼ **cups firmly packed light brown sugar**
  1 **egg**
⅓ **cup milk**
1½ **teaspoons vanilla**
  3 **cups quick oats, uncooked**
  1 **cup all-purpose flour**
½ **teaspoon baking soda**
½ **teaspoon salt**
¼ **teaspoon ground cinnamon**
  1 **cup chopped pecans**
⅔ **cup flake coconut**
⅔ **cup sesame seeds**

*Butter Flavor Crisco is artificially flavored.

1. Heat oven to 350°F. Grease baking sheets with shortening. Place sheets of foil on countertop for cooling cookies.

 2. Combine shortening, brown sugar, egg, milk and vanilla in large mixer bowl. Beat at medium speed of electric mixer until well blended.

3. Combine oats, flour, baking soda, salt and cinnamon. Mix into shortening mixture at low speed just until blended. Stir in pecans, coconut and sesame seeds.

4. Drop by rounded measuring tablespoonfuls of dough 2 inches apart onto prepared baking sheets.

5. Bake one baking sheet at a time at 375°F for 10 to 12 minutes or until lightly browned. *Do not overbake*. Remove cookies to foil to cool completely.   *Makes about 2½ dozen cookies*

Peanut Butter Chips and Jelly Bars

1½ **cups all-purpose flour**
½ **cup sugar**
¾ **teaspoon baking powder**
½ **cup (1 stick) cold butter or margarine**
  1 **egg, beaten**
¾ **cup grape jelly**
1⅔ **cups (10-ounce package) REESE'S®
   Peanut Butter Chips, divided**

Heat oven to 375°F. Grease 9-inch square baking pan. Stir together flour, sugar and baking powder. With pastry blender, cut in butter until mixture resembles coarse crumbs. Add egg; blend well. Reserve half of mixture; press remaining mixture onto bottom of prepared pan. Spread jelly over crust. Sprinkle 1 cup peanut butter chips over jelly. Stir together reserved crumb mixture with remaining ⅔ cup chips; sprinkle over top. Bake 25 to 30 minutes or until lightly browned. Cool completely in pan on wire rack. Cut into bars.

Makes about 16 bars

Peanut Butter Chips and Jelly Bars

Double Chocolate Banana Cookies

3 to 4 extra-ripe, medium DOLE® Bananas, peeled
2 cups rolled oats
2 cups sugar
1¾ cups all-purpose flour
½ cup unsweetened cocoa powder
1 teaspoon baking soda
½ teaspoon salt
2 eggs, slightly beaten
1¼ cups margarine, melted
1 cup DOLE® Chopped Natural Almonds, toasted
2 cups semisweet chocolate chips

• Purée bananas in blender; measure 2 cups for recipe.

• Combine oats, sugar, flour, cocoa, baking soda and salt until well mixed. Stir in bananas, eggs and margarine until blended. Stir in almonds and chocolate chips.

• Refrigerate batter 1 hour or until mixture becomes partially firm (batter runs during baking if too soft).

• Measure ¼ cup batter for each cookie; drop onto greased cookie sheet. Flatten slightly with spatula.

• Bake in 350°F oven 15 to 17 minutes until cookies are golden brown. Remove to wire rack to cool.   *Makes about 2½ dozen (3-inch) cookies*

Brownie Sandwich Cookies

BROWNIE COOKIES

1 package DUNCAN HINES® Double Fudge Brownie Mix
1 egg
3 tablespoons water
Sugar

FILLING

1 container (16 ounces) DUNCAN HINES® Creamy Homestyle Cream Cheese Frosting
Red food coloring (optional)
½ cup semisweet mini chocolate chips

1. Preheat oven to 375°F. Grease cookie sheets.

2. For brownie cookies, combine brownie mix, fudge packet from mix, egg and water in large bowl. Stir until well blended, about 50 strokes. Shape dough into 50 (1-inch) balls. Place 2 inches apart on prepared cookie sheets. Grease bottom of drinking glass; dip in sugar. Press gently to flatten 1 cookie to ⅜-inch thickness. Repeat with remaining cookies. Bake at 375°F for 6 to 7 minutes or until set. Cool 1 minute on cookie sheets. Remove to cooling racks. Cool completely.

3. For filling, tint frosting with red food coloring, if desired. Stir in chocolate chips.

4. To assemble, spread 1 tablespoon frosting on bottom of one cookie; top with second cookie. Press together to make sandwich cookie. Repeat with remaining cookies.

Makes 25 sandwich cookies

Brownie Sandwich Cookies

Sunflower Cookies in Flowerpots

¾ cup butter, softened
¼ cup granulated sugar
¼ cup packed light brown sugar
1 egg yolk
1⅓ cups all-purpose flour
¾ teaspoon baking powder
⅛ teaspoon salt
1 container (16 ounces) vanilla frosting
    Yellow food color
    Confectioners' sugar
1 gallon ice cream (any flavor), softened
    Brown decorating icing
24 chocolate sandwich cookies, crushed
1 cup shredded coconut, tinted green

SUPPLIES

3-inch fluted round cookie cutter
12 (6-inch) lollipop sticks
6 plastic drinking straws
12 (6½-ounce) paper cups
    Pastry bag and small writing tip
12 new (3¼-inch-diameter) ceramic
    flowerpots, about 3½ inches tall

1. Combine butter, granulated and brown sugars and egg yolk in medium bowl. Add flour, baking powder and salt; mix well. Cover; refrigerate about 4 hours or until firm.Preheat oven to 350°F. Grease cookie sheets.

2. On floured surface, roll dough to ⅛-inch thickness. Cut out cookies with fluted cookie cutter; place on prepared cookie sheets.

3. Bake 8 to 10 minutes or until edges are lightly browned. Remove to wire racks; cool completely.

4. Color vanilla frosting with yellow food color. Measure out ⅔ cup colored frosting; cover and set aside remaining frosting. Blend enough additional confectioners' sugar into measured ⅔ cup frosting to make a very thick frosting. Use about 1 tablespoon thickened frosting to attach lollipop stick to back of each cookie. Set aside to allow frosting to dry completely.

5. Cut straws crosswise in half. Hold 1 straw upright in center of each cup; pack ice cream around straw, completely filling each cup with ice cream. (Be sure straw sticks up out of ice cream.) Freeze until ice cream is hardened, 3 to 4 hours.

6. Frost front side of each cookie as desired with remaining frosting. Spoon brown icing into pastry bag fitted with writing tip; use to decorate cookies as shown in photo.

7. To serve, place cups filled with ice cream in flowerpots. Top with cookie crumbs to resemble dirt. Sprinkle tinted coconut around straw to resemble grass. Clip straw off to make it even with ice cream, taking care not to fill straw with crumbs or coconut. Insert lollipop stick, with cookie attached, into opening in each straw to stand cookie upright in flowerpot.

Makes 12 servings

Sunflower Cookies in Flowerpots

Bountiful BAR COOKIES

Choco-Lowfat Strawberry Shortbread Bars

¼ cup (½ stick) 60% vegetable oil spread
½ cup sugar
1 egg white
1¼ cups all-purpose flour
¼ cup HERSHEY'S Cocoa or HERSHEY'S
    Dutch Processed Cocoa
¾ teaspoon cream of tartar
½ teaspoon baking soda
    Dash salt
½ cup strawberry all-fruit spread
    White Chip Drizzle (recipe follows)

Heat oven to 375°F. Lightly spray 13×9×2-inch baking pan with vegetable cooking spray. Beat vegetable oil spread and sugar in medium bowl on medium speed of electric mixer until well blended. Add egg white; beat until well blended. Stir together flour, cocoa, cream of tartar, baking soda and salt; gradually add to sugar mixture, beating well. Gently press mixture onto bottom of prepared pan. Bake 10 to 12 minutes or just until set. Cool completely in pan on wire rack. Spread fruit spread evenly over crust. Cut into bars or other desired shapes with cookie cutters. Prepare White Chip Drizzle; drizzle over tops of bars. Let stand until set.   *Makes 36 bars*

White Chip Drizzle

⅓ cup HERSHEY'S Premier White Chips
½ teaspoon shortening (*do not use butter, margarine or oil*)

In small microwave-safe bowl, place white chips and shortening. Microwave at HIGH (100% power) 30 seconds; stir. If necessary, microwave at HIGH an additional 15 seconds at a time, stirring after each heating, just until chips are melted when stirred. Use immediately.

Nutrients per Serving (1 bar with drizzle):

Calories: 50, Total Fat: 1 g, Cholesterol: 0 mg, Sodium: 45 mg

Choco-Lowfat Strawberry Shortbread Bars

Marvelous Cookie Bars

½ cup (1 stick) butter or margarine, softened
1 cup firmly packed light brown sugar
2 large eggs
1⅓ cups all-purpose flour
1 cup quick-cooking or old-fashioned oats, uncooked
⅓ cup unsweetened cocoa powder
1 teaspoon baking powder
½ teaspoon salt
¼ teaspoon baking soda
½ cup chopped walnuts, divided
1 cup "M&M's"® Semi-Sweet Chocolate Mini Baking Bits, divided
½ cup cherry preserves
¼ cup shredded coconut

Preheat oven to 350°F. Lightly grease 9×9×2-inch baking pan; set aside. In large bowl cream butter and sugar until light and fluffy; beat in eggs. In medium bowl combine flour, oats, cocoa powder, baking powder, salt and baking soda; blend into creamed mixture. Stir in ¼ cup nuts and ¾ cup "M&M's"® Semi-Sweet Chocolate Mini Baking Bits. Reserve 1 cup dough; spread remaining dough into prepared pan. Combine preserves, coconut and remaining ¼ cup nuts; spread evenly over dough to within ½ inch of edge. Drop reserved dough by rounded teaspoonfuls over preserves mixture; sprinkle with remaining ¼ cup "M&M's"® Semi-Sweet Chocolate Mini Baking Bits. Bake 25 to 30 minutes or until slightly firm near edges. Cool completely. Cut into bars. Store in tightly covered container. *Makes 16 bars*

"Everything but the Kitchen Sink" Bar Cookies

1 package (18 ounces) refrigerated chocolate chip cookie dough
1 jar (7 ounces) marshmallow creme
½ cup creamy peanut butter
1½ cups toasted corn cereal
½ cup miniature candy-coated chocolate pieces

1. Preheat oven to 350°F. Grease 13×9-inch baking pan. Remove dough from wrapper according to package directions.

2. Press dough into prepared baking pan. Bake 13 minutes. Remove baking pan from oven. Drop teaspoonfuls of marshmallow cream and peanut butter over hot cookie base.

3. Bake 1 minute. Carefully spread marshmallow creme and peanut butter over cookie base. Sprinkle cereal and chocolate pieces over melted marshmallow and peanut butter mixture.

4. Bake 7 minutes. Cool completely on wire rack. Cut into 2-inch bars.

Makes 3 dozen bar cookies

"Everything but the Kitchen Sink" Bar Cookies

Fabulous Fruit Bars

1½ cups all-purpose flour, divided
1½ cups sugar, divided
½ cup MOTT'S® Apple Sauce, divided
½ teaspoon baking powder
2 tablespoons margarine
½ cup chopped peeled apple
½ cup chopped dried apricots
½ cup chopped cranberries
1 whole egg
1 egg white
1 teaspoon lemon juice
½ teaspoon vanilla extract
1 teaspoon ground cinnamon

1. Preheat oven to 350°F. Spray 13×9-inch baking pan with nonstick cooking spray.

2. In medium bowl, combine 1¼ cups flour, ½ cup sugar, ⅓ cup apple sauce and baking powder. Cut in margarine with pastry blender or fork until mixture resembles coarse crumbs.

3. In large bowl, combine apple, apricots, cranberries, remaining apple sauce, whole egg, egg white, lemon juice and vanilla.

4. In small bowl, combine remaining 1 cup sugar, ¼ cup flour and cinnamon. Add to fruit mixture, stirring just until mixed.

5. Press half of crumb mixture evenly into bottom of prepared pan. Top with fruit mixture. Sprinkle with remaining crumb mixture.

6. Bake 40 minutes or until lightly browned. Broil, 4 inches from heat, 1 to 2 minutes or until golden brown. Cool on wire rack 15 minutes; cut into bars. *Makes 16 servings*

Double Chocolate Fantasy Bars

2 cups chocolate cookie crumbs
⅓ cup (5⅓ tablespoons) butter or margarine, melted
1 (14-ounce) can sweetened condensed milk
1¾ cups "M&M's"® Semi-Sweet Chocolate Mini Baking Bits
1 cup shredded coconut
1 cup chopped walnuts or pecans

Preheat oven to 350°F. In large bowl combine cookie crumbs and butter; press mixture onto bottom of 13×9×2-inch baking pan. Pour condensed milk evenly over crumbs. Combine "M&M's"® Semi-Sweet Chocolate Mini Baking Bits, coconut and nuts. Sprinkle mixture evenly over condensed milk; press down lightly. Bake 25 to 30 minutes or until set. Cool completely. Cut into bars. Store in tightly covered container. *Makes 32 bars*

Fabulous Fruit Bars

Creative Pan Cookies

2¼ cups all-purpose flour
1 teaspoon baking soda
½ teaspoon salt
1 cup (2 sticks) butter, softened
¾ cup granulated sugar
¾ cup firmly packed brown sugar
1 teaspoon vanilla extract
2 eggs
2 cups (12-ounce package) NESTLÉ®
    TOLL HOUSE® Semi-Sweet Chocolate
    Morsels
Flavor Options, if desired (see below)

Preheat oven to 375°F. **COMBINE** flour, baking soda and salt in medium bowl. **BEAT** butter, granulated sugar, brown sugar and vanilla extract in large mixer bowl. Beat in eggs. Gradually beat in flour mixture. Stir in morsels and ingredients for one of the Flavor Options. Spread in ungreased 15½×10½×1-inch baking pan.

BAKE in preheated 375°F. oven18 to 20 minutes. Cool completely in pan on wire rack. Cut into 2-inch squares.   *Makes 35 squares*

Granola-Nut Cookies: Stir in 2 cups granola cereal, 1 cup raisins and 1 cup chopped walnuts.

Apricot-Cashew Cookies: Stir in 2 cups granola cereal, 1 cup chopped dried apricots and 1 cup chopped dry-roasted cashews.

Apple-Oatmeal Cookies: Decrease all-purpose flour to 2 cups. Stir in 2¼ cups quick oats, uncooked, 1 cup diced peeled apples and ¾ teaspoon cinnamon.

Carrot-Pineapple Cookies: Increase all-purpose flour to 2¾ cups. Add ½ teaspoon cinnamon and ¼ teaspoon *each* allspice and nutmeg. Stir in 1 cup grated carrots, 1 (8 ounce) can juice-packed crushed pineapple, well drained, and ¾ cup wheat germ.   *Makes 20 bars*

No-Fuss Bar Cookies

24 graham cracker squares
1 cup semisweet chocolate chips
1 cup flaked coconut
¾ cup coarsely chopped walnuts
1 can (14 ounces) sweetened condensed
    milk

1. Preheat oven to 350°F. Grease 13×9-inch baking pan; set aside.

2. Place graham crackers in food processor. Process until crackers form fine crumbs. Measure 2 cups of crumbs. Combine crumbs, chips, coconut and walnuts in medium bowl; stir to blend. Add milk; stir with spoon until blended.

3. Spread batter evenly into prepared pan. Bake 15 to 18 minutes or until edges are golden brown. Let pan stand on wire rack until completely cooled. Cut into 2¼×2¼-inch bars.

Makes 20 bars

Coconut Pecan Bars

1¼ cups granulated sugar, divided
½ cup plus 3 tablespoons all-purpose flour,
    divided
1½ cups finely chopped pecans, divided
¾ cup (1½ sticks) butter or margarine,
    softened, divided
2 large eggs
1 tablespoon vanilla extract
1¾ cups "M&M's"® Chocolate Mini Baking
    Bits, divided
1 cup shredded coconut

Preheat oven to 350°F. Lightly grease 13×9×2-inch baking pan; set aside. In large bowl combine ¾ cup sugar, ½ cup flour and ½ cup nuts; add ¼ cup melted butter and mix well. Press mixture onto bottom of prepared pan. Bake 10 minutes or until set; cool slightly. In large bowl cream remaining ½ cup butter and ½ cup sugar; beat in eggs and vanilla. Combine 1 cup "M&M's"® Chocolate Mini Baking Bits and remaining 3 tablespoons flour; stir into creamed mixture. Spread mixture over cooled crust. Combine coconut and remaining 1 cup nuts; sprinkle over batter. Sprinkle remaining ¾ cup "M&M's"® Chocolate Mini Baking Bits over coconut and nuts; pat down lightly. Bake 25 to 30 minutes or until set. Cool completely. Cut into bars. Store in tightly covered container. *Makes 24 bars*

Butterscotch Pan Cookies

1 package DUNCAN HINES® Moist
    Deluxe French Vanilla Cake Mix
1 cup butter or margarine, melted
2 eggs
¾ cup firmly packed light brown sugar
1 teaspoon vanilla extract
1 package (12 ounces) butterscotch flavored
    chips
1½ cups chopped pecans

1. Preheat oven to 375°F. Grease 15½×10½×1-inch jelly-roll pan.

2. Combine cake mix, melted butter, eggs, brown sugar and vanilla extract in large bowl. Beat at low speed with electric mixer until smooth and creamy. Stir in butterscotch chips and pecans. Spread in pan. Bake at 375°F for 20 to 25 minutes or until golden brown. Cool completely. Cut into bars. *Makes 48 bars*

Tip: You can substitute chocolate or peanut butter flavored chips for the butterscotch flavored chips.

Crispy Cocoa Bars

¼ cup (½ stick) margarine
¼ cup HERSHEY'S Cocoa
5 cups miniature marshmallows
5 cups crisp rice cereal

Spray 13×9×2-inch pan with vegetable cooking spray. Melt margarine in large saucepan over low heat; stir in cocoa and marshmallows. Cook over low heat, stirring constantly, until marshmallows are melted and mixture is smooth and well blended. Continue cooking 1 minute, stirring constantly. Remove from heat. Add cereal; stir until coated. Lightly spray spatula with vegetable cooking spray; press mixture into prepared pan. Cool completely. Cut into bars.   *Makes 24 bars*

Applesauce Fudge Bars

   3 squares (1 ounce *each*) semisweet
      chocolate
½ cup butter
⅔ cup unsweetened applesauce
   2 eggs, beaten
   1 cup packed light brown sugar
   1 teaspoon vanilla
   1 cup all-purpose flour
½ teaspoon baking powder
¼ teaspoon baking soda
½ cup walnuts, chopped
   1 cup (6 ounces) milk chocolate chips

Preheat oven to 350°F. Grease 9-inch square pan. Melt semisweet chocolate and butter in small heavy saucepan over low heat. Remove from heat; cool. Combine applesauce, eggs, sugar and vanilla in large bowl. Combine flour, baking powder and baking soda in small bowl. Mix dry ingredients into applesauce mixture; blend in chocolate mixture. Spread batter evenly in prepared pan. Sprinkle nuts over top. Bake 25 to 30 minutes or just until set. Remove from oven; sprinkle chocolate chips over the top. Let stand until chips melt; spread evenly over bars. Cool in pan on wire rack. Cut into 2-inch bars.

Makes about 3 dozen bars

Lemon Bars

CRUST
   1 cup all-purpose flour
½ cup powdered sugar
¼ cup MOTT'S® Natural Apple Sauce
   2 tablespoons margarine, melted

LEMON FILLING
   1 cup granulated sugar
   2 egg whites
   1 whole egg
⅓ cup MOTT'S® Natural Apple Sauce
   1 teaspoon grated lemon peel
¼ cup lemon juice
   3 tablespoons all-purpose flour
½ teaspoon baking powder
      Additional powdered sugar (optional)

1. Preheat oven to 350°F. Spray 8-inch square baking pan with nonstick cooking spray.

2. To prepare Crust, in small bowl, combine 1 cup flour and powdered sugar. Add ¼ cup apple sauce and margarine. Stir with fork until mixture resembles coarse crumbs. Press evenly into bottom of prepared pan. Bake 10 minutes.

3. To prepare Lemon Filling, in medium bowl, beat granulated sugar, egg whites and whole egg with electric mixer at medium speed until thick and smooth. Add ⅓ cup apple sauce, lemon peel, lemon juice, 3 tablespoons flour and baking powder. Beat until well blended. Pour lemon filling over baked crust.

4. Bake 20 to 25 minutes or until lightly browned. Cool completely on wire rack. Sprinkle with additional powdered sugar, if desired; cut into 14 bars.   *Makes 14 servings*

Fruit and Oat Squares

1 cup all-purpose flour
1 cup uncooked quick oats
¾ cup packed light brown sugar
½ teaspoon baking soda
¼ teaspoon salt
¼ teaspoon ground cinnamon
⅓ cup butter, melted
¾ cup apricot, cherry or other fruit flavor
   preserves

1. Preheat oven to 350°F. Spray 9-inch square baking pan with nonstick cooking spray; set aside.

2. Combine flour, oats, brown sugar, baking soda, salt and cinnamon in medium bowl; mix well. Add butter; stir with fork until mixture is crumbly. Reserve ¾ cup crumb mixture for topping. Press remaining crumb mixture evenly onto bottom of prepared pan. Bake 5 to 7 minutes or until lightly browned. Spread preserves onto crust; sprinkle with reserved crumb mixture.

3. Bake 20 to 25 minutes or until golden brown. Cool completely in pan on wire rack. Cut into 16 squares. *Makes 16 servings*

Rainbow Blondies

1 cup (2 sticks) butter or margarine,
   softened
1½ cups firmly packed light brown sugar
1 large egg
1 teaspoon vanilla extract
2 cups all-purpose flour
½ teaspoon baking soda
1¾ cups "M&M's"® Semi-Sweet or Milk
   Chocolate Mini Baking Bits
1 cup chopped walnuts or pecans

Preheat oven to 350°F. Lightly grease 13×9×2-inch baking pan; set aside. In large bowl cream butter and sugar until light and fluffy; beat in egg and vanilla. In medium bowl combine flour and baking soda; add to creamed mixture just until combined. Dough will be stiff. Stir in "M&M's"® Chocolate Mini Baking Bits and nuts. Spread dough into prepared baking pan. Bake 30 to 35 minutes or until toothpick inserted in center comes out with moist crumbs. *Do not overbake.* Cool completely. Cut into bars. Store in tightly covered container. *Makes 24 bars*

Fruit and Oat Squares

Tri-Layer Chocolate Oatmeal Bars

CRUST

- 1 cup uncooked rolled oats
- ½ cup all-purpose flour
- ½ cup firmly packed light brown sugar
- ¼ cup MOTT'S® Natural Apple Sauce
- 1 tablespoon margarine, melted
- ¼ teaspoon baking soda

FILLING

- ⅔ cup all-purpose flour
- ½ teaspoon baking powder
- ¼ teaspoon salt
- ¾ cup granulated sugar
- ¼ cup MOTT'S® Natural Apple Sauce
- 1 whole egg
- 1 egg white
- 2 tablespoons unsweetened cocoa powder
- 1 tablespoon margarine, melted
- ½ teaspoon vanilla extract
- ¼ cup low-fat buttermilk

ICING

- 1 cup powdered sugar
- 1 tablespoon unsweetened cocoa powder
- 1 tablespoon skim milk
- 1 teaspoon instant coffee powder

1. Preheat oven to 350°F. Spray 8-inch square baking pan with nonstick cooking spray.

2. To prepare Crust, in medium bowl, combine oats, ½ cup flour, brown sugar, ¼ cup apple sauce, 1 tablespoon margarine and baking soda. Stir with fork until mixture resembles coarse crumbs. Press evenly into bottom of prepared pan. Bake 10 minutes.

3. To prepare Filling, in small bowl, combine ⅔ cup flour, baking powder and salt.

4. In large bowl, combine granulated sugar, ¼ cup apple sauce, whole egg, egg white, 2 tablespoons cocoa, 1 tablespoon margarine and vanilla.

5. Add flour mixture to apple sauce mixture alternately with buttermilk; stir until well blended. Spread filling over baked crust.

6. Bake 25 minutes or until toothpick inserted in center comes out clean. Cool completely on wire rack.

7. To prepare Icing, in small bowl, combine powdered sugar, 1 tablespoon cocoa, milk and coffee powder until smooth. Spread evenly over bars. Let stand until set. Run tip of knife through icing to score. Cut into 14 bars.

Makes 14 servings

Tri-Layer Chocolate Oatmeal Bars

Chocolate Oat Shortbread

1 cup (2 sticks) butter, softened
1 cup powdered sugar
2 teaspoons vanilla extract
1½ cups all-purpose flour
1 cup quick-cooking or old-fashioned oats, uncooked
¼ cup unsweetened cocoa powder
1 teaspoon ground cinnamon
1¾ cups "M&M's"® Chocolate Mini Baking Bits, divided

Preheat oven to 325°F. Lightly grease 13×9×2-inch pan. Cream butter and sugar until light and fluffy; add vanilla. Combine flour, oats, cocoa powder and cinnamon; blend into creamed mixture. Stir in 1 cup baking bits; press dough into prepared pan. Sprinkle remaining ¾ cup baking bits over dough; press in lightly. Bake 20 to 25 minutes or until set. Cool completely; cut into triangles.   *Makes 36 to 48 bars*

Colorful Caramel Bites

1 cup plus 6 tablespoons all-purpose flour, divided
1 cup quick-cooking or old-fashioned oats, uncooked
¾ cup firmly packed light brown sugar
½ teaspoon baking soda
¼ teaspoon salt
¾ cup (1½ sticks) butter or margarine, melted
1¾ cups "M&M's"® Semi-Sweet Chocolate Mini Baking Bits, divided
1½ cups chopped pecans, divided
1 jar (12 ounces) caramel ice cream topping

Preheat oven to 350°F. Combine 1 cup flour, oats, sugar, baking soda and salt; blend in melted butter to form crumbly mixture. Press half the crumb mixture onto bottom of 9×9×2-inch baking pan; bake 10 minutes. Sprinkle with 1 cup "M&M's"® Semi-Sweet Chocolate Mini Baking Bits and 1 cup nuts. Blend remaining 6 tablespoons flour with caramel topping; pour over top. Combine remaining crumb mixture, remaining ¾ cup "M&M's"® Semi-Sweet Chocolate Mini Baking Bits and remaining ½ cup nuts; sprinkle over caramel layer. Bake 20 to 25 minutes or until golden brown. Cool completely. Cut into squares.   *Makes 36 bars*

Top to bottom: Colorful Caramel Bites and Chocolate Oat Shortbread

Fruit and Nut Bars

    1 cup unsifted all-purpose flour
    1 cup quick oats
    ⅔ cup brown sugar
    2 teaspoons baking soda
    ½ teaspoon salt
    ½ teaspoon cinnamon
    ⅔ cup buttermilk
    3 tablespoons vegetable oil
    2 egg whites, lightly beaten
    1 Washington Golden Delicious apple, cored
        and chopped
    ½ cup dried cranberries or raisins, chopped
    ¼ cup chopped nuts
    2 tablespoons flaked coconut (optional)

1. Heat oven to 375°F. Lightly grease 9-inch square baking pan. In large mixing bowl, combine flour, oats, brown sugar, baking soda, salt and cinnamon; stir to blend.

2. Add buttermilk, oil and egg whites; beat with electric mixer just until mixed. Stir in apple, dried fruit and nuts; spread evenly in pan and top with coconut, if desired. Bake 20 to 25 minutes or until cake tester inserted in center comes out clean. Cool and cut into 10 bars.

Makes 10 bars

Favorite recipe from **Washington Apple Commission**

Oatmeal Brownie Gems

    2¾ cups quick-cooking or old-fashioned oats,
        uncooked
    1 cup all-purpose flour
    1 cup firmly packed light brown sugar
    1 cup coarsely chopped walnuts
    1 teaspoon baking soda
    1 cup (2 sticks) butter or margarine, melted
    1¾ cups "M&M's"® Semi-Sweet Chocolate
        Mini Baking Bits
    1 (19- to 21-ounce) package fudge brownie
        mix, prepared according to package
        directions for fudge-like brownies

Preheat oven to 350°F. In large bowl combine oats, flour, sugar, nuts and baking soda; add butter until mixture forms coarse crumbs. Toss in "M&M's"® Semi-Sweet Chocolate Mini Baking Bits until evenly distributed. Reserve 3 cups mixture. Pat remaining mixture onto bottom of 15×10×1-inch pan to form crust. Pour prepared brownie mix over crust, carefully spreading into thin layer. Sprinkle reserved crumb mixture over top of brownie mixture; pat down lightly. Bake 25 to 30 minutes or until toothpick inserted in center comes out with moist crumbs. Cool completely. Cut into bars. Store in tightly covered container.

Makes 48 bars

Fruit and Nut Bars

Chocolate Orange Gems

⅔ cup butter-flavored solid vegetable
   shortening
¾ cup firmly packed light brown sugar
1 large egg
¼ cup orange juice
1 tablespoon grated orange zest
2¼ cups all-purpose flour
½ teaspoon baking powder
½ teaspoon baking soda
½ teaspoon salt
1¾ cups "M&M's"® Chocolate Mini Baking
   Bits
1 cup coarsely chopped pecans
⅓ cup orange marmalade
   Vanilla Glaze (recipe follows)

Preheat oven to 350°F. In large bowl cream
shortening and sugar until light and fluffy; beat in
egg, orange juice and orange zest. In medium
bowl combine flour, baking powder, baking soda
and salt; blend into creamed mixture. Stir in
"M&M's"® Chocolate Mini Baking Bits and nuts.
Reserve 1 cup dough; spread remaining dough
into ungreased 13×9×2-inch baking pan. Spread
marmalade evenly over top of dough to within
½ inch of edges. Drop reserved dough by
teaspoonfuls randomly over marmalade. Bake 25
to 30 minutes or until light golden brown. *Do not
overbake.* Cool completely; drizzle with Vanilla
Glaze. Cut into bars. Store in tightly covered
container.   *Makes 24 bars*

Vanilla Glaze: Combine 1 cup powdered sugar
and 1 to 1½ tablespoons warm water until desired
consistency. Place glaze in resealable plastic
sandwich bag; seal bag. Cut a tiny piece off one
corner of the bag (not more than ⅛ inch). Drizzle
glaze over cookies.

Chewy Bar Cookies

½ cup margarine, softened
1 cup firmly packed light brown sugar
2 eggs
3 (1¼-ounce) packages Instant CREAM OF
   WHEAT® Cereal Apple 'n Cinnamon
   Flavor
⅔ cup all-purpose flour
2 teaspoons baking powder
1 cup PLANTERS® Walnuts, finely
   chopped

Preheat oven to 350°F. In large bowl, with
electric mixer at medium speed, beat margarine
and brown sugar until creamy. Beat in eggs until
light and fluffy. Stir in cereal, flour and baking
powder. Mix in walnuts. Spread batter in greased
15½×10½×1-inch baking pan.

Bake 20 to 25 minutes or until golden brown.
Cool completely in pan on wire rack. Cut
into bars.   *Makes about 48 bars*

Chocolate Orange Gems

Amazing ELEGANT TREASURES

Chocolate Edged Lace Cookies

⅔ cup ground almonds
½ cup butter
½ cup sugar
2 tablespoons milk
1 tablespoon flour
4 ounces dark sweet or bittersweet chocolate candy bar, broken into pieces

Preheat oven to 325°F. Grease cookie sheets very lightly. Combine almonds, butter, sugar, milk and flour in large skillet. Cook and stir over low heat until well blended. Keep mixture warm over very low heat while forming and baking cookies.

Drop tablespoonfuls of batter 2 inches apart on prepared cookie sheets. Bake 6 minutes or until cookies are golden brown. Let cookies stand on cookie sheets 30 seconds to 1 minute before loosening with thin spatula. (If cookies become too brittle to remove, warm them briefly in oven.) Remove cookies to wire rack;* cool.

Melt chocolate in small, heavy saucepan over low heat, stirring constantly. Tilt saucepan to pool chocolate at one end; dip edge of each cookie in chocolate, turning cookie slowly so entire edge is tinged with chocolate. Let cookies stand on waxed paper until chocolate is set.

Makes about 2 dozen cookies

*For tuile-shaped cookies, balance a wooden spoon over two cans of the same height. Working quickly while cookies are still hot, drape the cookies (bottom side down) over the handle of the spoon so that both sides hang down and form a taco shape. When firm, transfer to wire rack to cool completely. Dip both edges of cooled cookies into chocolate.

Chocolate Edged Lace Cookies

Raspberry Almond Sandwich Cookies

1 package DUNCAN HINES® Golden
    Sugar Cookie Mix
1 egg
¼ cup CRISCO® Oil or CRISCO®
    PURITAN® Canola Oil
1 tablespoon water
¾ teaspoon almond extract
1⅓ cups sliced natural almonds, broken
    Seedless red raspberry jam

1. Preheat oven to 375°F.

2. Combine cookie mix, egg, oil, water and almond extract in large bowl. Stir until thoroughly blended. Drop half of dough by level measuring teaspoonfuls 2 inches apart onto ungreased cookie sheets. (It is a small amount of dough but will spread during baking to 1½ to 1¾ inches.)

3. Place almonds on waxed paper. Drop other half of dough by level measuring teaspoonfuls onto nuts. Place, almond-side-up, 2 inches apart on cookie sheets.

4. Bake both plain and almond cookies at 375°F for 6 minutes or until set but not browned. Cool 1 minute on cookie sheets. Remove to cooling racks. Cool completely.

5. Spread bottoms of plain cookies with jam; top with almond cookies. Press together to make sandwiches. Store in airtight container.

Makes 6 dozen sandwich cookies

Milk Chocolate Florentine Cookies

⅔ cup butter
2 cups quick oats, uncooked
1 cup granulated sugar
⅔ cup all-purpose flour
¼ cup light or dark corn syrup
¼ cup milk
1 teaspoon vanilla extract
¼ teaspoon salt
2 cups (11.5-ounce package) NESTLÉ®
    TOLL HOUSE® Milk Chocolate
    Morsels

MELT butter in medium saucepan; remove from heat. Stir in oats, sugar, flour, corn syrup, milk, vanilla extract and salt; mix well. Drop by level teaspoonfuls, about 3 inches apart, onto foil-lined baking sheets. Spread thinly with rubber spatula.

BAKE in preheated 375°F. oven for 6 to 8 minutes until golden brown; cool on baking sheets on wire racks. Peel foil from cookies.

MICROWAVE morsels in medium microwave-safe bowl on MEDIUM HIGH (70%) power for 1 minute; stir. Microwave at additional 10- to 20-second intervals, stirring until smooth. Spread thin layer of melted chocolate on flat side of *half* the cookies. Top with remaining cookies.

Makes about 3½ dozen sandwich cookies

Raspberry Almond Sandwich Cookies

White Chocolate Chunk & Macadamia Nut Brownie Cookies

1½ cups firmly packed light brown sugar
⅔ cup CRISCO® Stick or ⅔ CRISCO®
    all-vegetable shortening
1 tablespoon water
1 teaspoon vanilla
2 eggs
1½ cups all-purpose flour
⅓ cup unsweetened cocoa powder
½ teaspoon salt
¼ teaspoon baking soda
1 cup white chocolate chunks or chips
1 cup coarsely chopped macadamia nuts

1. Heat oven to 375°F. Place sheets of foil on countertop for cooling cookies.

2. Place brown sugar, shortening, water and vanilla in large bowl. Beat at medium speed of electric mixer until well blended. Add eggs; beat well.

3. Combine flour, cocoa, salt and baking soda. Add to shortening mixture; beat at low speed just until blended. Stir in white chocolate chunks and macadamia nuts.

4. Drop dough by rounded measuring tablespoonfuls 2 inches apart onto ungreased baking sheet.

5. Bake one baking sheet at a time at 375°F for 7 to 9 minutes or until cookies are set. *Do not overbake*. Cool 2 minutes on baking sheet. Remove cookies to foil to cool completely.
Makes about 3 dozen cookies

Chocolate & Peanut Butter Tweed Cookies

1 cup butter, softened
½ cup packed light brown sugar
¼ cup granulated sugar
1 egg
¼ teaspoon baking soda
2½ cups all-purpose flour
½ cup *each* semisweet chocolate chips and
    peanut butter chips, chopped*

*Chips can be chopped in food processor.

Beat butter and sugars in large bowl with electric mixer until smooth. Add egg and baking soda; beat until light and fluffy. Stir in flour until dough is smooth. Blend in chopped chips. Divide dough into 4 parts. Shape each part into a roll, about 1½ inches in diameter. Wrap in plastic wrap; refrigerate until firm, at least 1 hour or up to 2 weeks.

Preheat oven to 375°F. Lightly grease cookie sheets or line with parchment paper. Cut rolls into ⅛-inch-thick slices; place 2 inches apart on prepared cookie sheets. Bake 10 to 12 minutes or until lightly browned. Remove to wire racks to cool. *Makes about 6 dozen cookies*

White Chocolate Chunk &
Macadamia Nut Brownie Cookies

Caramel Lace Chocolate Chip Cookies

½ cup light corn syrup
¼ **Butter Flavor* CRISCO® Stick or ¼ cup Butter Flavor* CRISCO® all-vegetable shortening**
1 tablespoon brown sugar
1½ teaspoons grated orange peel (optional)
½ teaspoon vanilla
½ cup all-purpose flour
¼ teaspoon salt
⅓ cup semi-sweet chocolate chips
⅓ cup coarsely chopped pecans

*Butter Flavor Crisco is artificially flavored.

1. Heat oven to 375°F. Grease baking sheets with shortening. Place foil on countertop for cooling cookies.

2. Combine corn syrup, shortening, brown sugar, orange peel and vanilla in large bowl. Beat at medium speed of electric mixer until well blended.

3. Combine flour and salt. Mix into creamed mixture at low speed until blended. Stir in chocolate chips and nuts. Drop teaspoonfuls of dough 4 inches apart onto baking sheets.

4. Bake one baking sheet at a time at 375°F for 5 minutes or until edges are golden brown. (Chips and nuts will remain in center while dough spreads out.) *Do not overbake.* Cool 2 minutes on baking sheets. Lift each cookie edge with spatula. Grasp cookie edge gently and lightly pinch or flute the edge, bringing it up to chips and nuts in center. Work around each cookie until completely fluted. Remove cookies to foil to cool completely.

Makes about 3 dozen cookies

Almond Raspberry Thumbprint Cookies

1 cup butter or margarine, softened
1 cup sugar
1 can SOLO® or 1 jar BAKER® Almond Filling
2 egg yolks
1 teaspoon almond extract
2½ cups all-purpose flour
½ teaspoon baking powder
½ teaspoon salt
1 can SOLO® or 1 jar BAKER® Raspberry or Strawberry FILLING

Beat butter and sugar in medium bowl with electric mixer until light and fluffy. Add almond filling, egg yolks and almond extract; beat until blended. Stir in flour, baking powder and salt with wooden spoon to make soft dough. Cover and refrigerate at least 3 hours or overnight.

Preheat oven to 350°F. Shape dough into 1-inch balls. Place 1½ inches apart on ungreased cookie sheets. Press thumb into center of each ball to make deep depression. Spoon ½ teaspoon raspberry filling into depressions.

Bake 11 to 13 minutes or until edges of cookies are golden brown. Cool on cookie sheets 1 minute. Remove to wire racks; cool completely.

Makes about 60 cookies

Caramel Lace Chocolate Chip Cookies

Chocolate Macadamia Chewies

¾ cup (1½ sticks) butter or margarine,
    softened
⅔ cup firmly packed light brown sugar
1 large egg
1 teaspoon vanilla extract
1¾ cups all-purpose flour
¾ teaspoon baking soda
¼ teaspoon salt
¾ cup (3½ ounces) coarsely chopped
    macadamia nuts
½ cup shredded coconut
1¾ cups "M&M's"® Chocolate Mini Baking
    Bits

Preheat oven to 350°F. In large bowl cream
butter and sugar until light and fluffy; beat in egg
and vanilla. In medium bowl combine flour,
baking soda and salt; blend into creamed
mixture. Blend in nuts and coconut. Stir in
"M&M's"® Chocolate Mini Baking Bits. Drop by
heaping teaspoonfuls about 2 inches apart onto
ungreased cookie sheets; flatten slightly with
back of spoon. Bake 8 to 10 minutes or until set.
Do not overbake. Cool 1 minute on cookie sheets;
cool completely on wire racks. Store in tightly
covered container.

Makes about 4 dozen cookies

Brandy Lace Cookies

¼ cup sugar
¼ cup MAZOLA® Margarine
¼ cup KARO® Light or Dark Corn Syrup
½ cup all-purpose flour
¼ cup very finely chopped pecans or walnuts
2 tablespoons brandy
    Melted white and/or semisweet chocolate
    (optional)

1. Preheat oven to 350°F. Lightly grease and flour
cookie sheets.

2. In small saucepan, combine sugar, margarine
and corn syrup. Bring to a boil over medium heat,
stirring constantly. Remove from heat. Stir in
flour, pecans and brandy. Drop 12 half
teaspoonfuls of batter 2 inches apart onto
prepared cookie sheets.

3. Bake 6 minutes or until golden. Cool 1 to
2 minutes or until cookies can be lifted but are
still warm and soft. Remove cookies with spatula.
Curl cookies around handle of wooden spoon;
slide off when crisp. If cookies harden before
curling, return to oven to soften.

4. If desired, drizzle with melted chocolate.

Makes 4 to 5 dozen cookies

Prep Time: 30 minutes
Bake Time: 6 minutes, plus curling and cooling

Chocolate Macadamia Chewies

Double-Dipped Chocolate Peanut Butter Cookies

1¼ cups all-purpose flour
½ teaspoon baking powder
½ teaspoon baking soda
½ teaspoon salt
½ cup butter, softened
½ cup granulated sugar
½ cup packed light brown sugar
½ cup creamy or chunky peanut butter
1 egg
1 teaspoon vanilla
   Additional granulated sugar
1½ cups semisweet chocolate chips
1½ cups milk chocolate chips
3 teaspoons shortening, divided

1. Preheat oven to 350°F.

2. Combine flour, baking powder, baking soda and salt in small bowl.

3. Beat butter, ½ cup granulated sugar and brown sugar in large bowl with electric mixer at medium speed until light and fluffy. Beat in peanut butter, egg and vanilla. Gradually stir in flour mixture blending well.

4. Roll heaping tablespoonfuls of dough into 1½-inch balls. Place balls 2 inches apart on ungreased cookie sheets. (If dough is too soft to roll into balls, refrigerate 30 minutes.)

5. Dip fork into additional granulated sugar; press criss-cross fashion onto each ball, flattening to ½-inch thickness.

6. Bake 12 minutes or until set. Let cookies stand on cookie sheets 2 minutes. Remove cookies to wire rack; cool completely.

7. Melt semisweet chocolate chips and 1½ teaspoons shortening in top of double boiler over hot, not boiling, water.

8. Dip one end of each cookie one third the way up; place on waxed paper. Let stand until chocolate is set, about 30 minutes.

9. Melt milk chocolate chips with remaining 1½ teaspoons shortening in top of double boiler over hot, not boiling, water.

10. Dip opposite end of each cookie one third the way up; place on waxed paper. Let stand until chocolate is set, about 30 minutes.

11. Store cookies between sheets of waxed paper at cool room temperature or freeze up to 3 months.   *Makes about 2 dozen (3-inch) cookies*

*Double-Dipped Chocolate
Peanut Butter Cookies*

Jam-Up Oatmeal Cookies

1 Butter Flavor* CRISCO® Stick or 1 cup
    Butter Flavor* CRISCO® all-vegetable
    shortening
1½ cups firmly packed brown sugar
2 eggs
2 teaspoons almond extract
2 cups all-purpose flour
1 teaspoon baking powder
1 teaspoon salt
½ teaspoon baking soda
2½ cups uncooked quick oats (not instant or
    old fashioned)
1 cup finely chopped pecans
1 jar (12 ounces) strawberry jam
    Sugar for sprinkling

*Butter Flavor Crisco is artificially flavored.

1. Combine shortening and brown sugar in large bowl. Beat at medium speed of electric mixer until well blended. Beat in eggs and almond extract.

2. Combine flour, baking powder, salt and baking soda. Mix into shortening mixture at low speed until just blended. Stir in oats and chopped nuts with spoon. Cover and refrigerate at least 1 hour.

3. Heat oven to 350°F. Grease baking sheets with shortening. Place sheets of foil on countertop for cooling cookies.

4. Roll out dough, half at a time, to about ¼-inch thickness on floured surface. Cut out with 2½-inch round cookie cutter. Place 1 teaspoonful of jam in center of half of the rounds. Top with remaining rounds. Press edges to seal. Prick centers; sprinkle with sugar. Place 1 inch apart on baking sheets.

5. Bake one baking sheet at a time at 350°F for 12 to 15 minutes or until lightly browned. *Do not overbake.* Cool 2 minutes on baking sheets. Remove cookies to foil to cool completely.

Makes about 2 dozen cookies

Peanut Butter Brickle Cookies

1½ cups all-purpose flour
1 cup granulated sugar
1 cup butter, softened
½ cup peanut butter
2 tablespoons packed light brown sugar
1 egg
½ teaspoon baking soda
1 teaspoon vanilla
1 package (6 ounces) almond brickle bits

Preheat oven to 350°F. Grease cookie sheets. Combine flour, granulated sugar, butter, peanut butter, brown sugar, egg, baking soda and vanilla in large bowl. Beat at medium speed of electric mixer until well blended, 2 to 3 minutes. Stir in almond brickle bits.

Shape rounded teaspoonfuls of dough into 1-inch balls. Place 2 inches apart on prepared cookie sheets. Flatten cookies to ⅛-inch thickness with bottom of glass covered with waxed paper. Bake 7 to 9 minutes or until edges are very lightly browned.

Makes about 4 dozen cookies

Jam-Up Oatmeal Cookies

Orange & Chocolate Ribbon Cookies

1 cup butter, softened
½ cup sugar
3 egg yolks
2 teaspoons grated orange peel
1 teaspoon orange extract
2¼ cups all-purpose flour, divided
3 tablespoons unsweetened cocoa powder
1 teaspoon vanilla
1 teaspoon chocolate extract

Beat butter, sugar and egg yolks in large bowl until light and fluffy. Remove half of mixture; place in another bowl. Add orange peel, orange extract and 1¼ cups flour to one half of mixture; mix until blended and smooth. Shape into a ball. Add cocoa, vanilla and chocolate extract to second half of mixture; beat until smooth. Stir in remaining 1 cup flour; mix until blended. Shape into a ball. Cover dough; chill 10 minutes.

Roll out each dough separately on lightly floured surface to 12×4-inch rectangle. Place one dough on top of the other. Using knife, make lengthwise cut through center of doughs. Lift half of dough onto other to make long, 4-layer strip of dough. Press dough strips together. Wrap in plastic wrap; refrigerate 1 hour.

Preheat oven to 350°F. Lightly grease cookie sheets or line with parchment paper. Cut dough crosswise into ¼-inch-thick slices; place 2 inches apart on cookie sheets. Bake 10 to 12 minutes or until lightly browned. Cool on wire racks.

Makes about 5 dozen cookies

Chocolate Mousse Squares

¾ cup plus 2 tablespoons all-purpose flour, divided
⅔ cup plus 3 tablespoons granulated sugar, divided
¼ cup (½ stick) cold margarine
¼ cup HERSHEY'S Cocoa
½ teaspoon powdered instant coffee
¼ teaspoon baking powder
½ cup liquid egg substitute
½ teaspoon vanilla extract
½ cup plain lowfat yogurt
½ teaspoon powdered sugar

Heat oven to 350°F. Stir together ¾ cup flour and 3 tablespoons granulated sugar. With pastry blender or 2 knives, cut in margarine until fine crumbs form. Press mixture onto bottom of ungreased 8-inch square baking pan. Bake 15 minutes or until golden. *Reduce oven temperature to 300°F.*

Stir together remaining ⅔ cup granulated sugar, cocoa, remaining 2 tablespoons flour, instant coffee and baking powder. Add egg substitute and vanilla; beat on medium speed of electric mixer until well blended. Add yogurt; beat just until blended. Pour over prepared crust.

Bake 30 minutes or until center is set. Cool completely in pan on wire rack. Cut into squares. If desired, place small paper cutouts over top. Sift powdered sugar over cutouts. Carefully remove cutouts. Store covered in refrigerator.

Makes 16 squares

Chocolate Mousse Squares

Pecan Toffee Filled Ravioli Cookies

FILLING

    1 cup packed brown sugar
    1/4 cup butter, melted
    1/2 cup chopped pecans
    2 tablespoons all-purpose flour

BUTTER DOUGH

  1 1/2 cups butter, softened
    1/2 cup granulated sugar
    1/2 cup packed light brown sugar
    2 egg yolks
  2 1/2 cups all-purpose flour
  1 1/2 teaspoons baking powder
    1/4 teaspoon salt

1. For Filling, stir brown sugar into melted butter in large bowl until well blended. Add pecans and flour; mix well.

2. Transfer filling to waxed paper; shape into 7-inch square. Cut into 36 (1 1/4-inch) pieces. Refrigerate 1 hour or overnight.

3. For Butter Dough combine butter, sugars and egg yolk in medium bowl. Add flour, baking powder and salt; mix well. Cover; refrigerate about 4 hours or until firm. Roll half of dough on well-floured sheet of waxed paper to 12-inch square.

4. Repeat with second half of dough. If dough becomes soft, refrigerate 1 hour.

5. Preheat oven to 350°F. Lightly score 1 layer of dough at 2 inch intervals to form 36 squares. Place 1 square of filling in center of each square.

6. Carefully place second layer of dough over filling. Press gently between rows. Cut with knife, ravioli wheel or pastry cutter. Transfer filled ravioli to ungreased cookie sheets.

7. Bake 14 to 16 minutes or until lightly browned. Cool on cookie sheets 5 minutes. Remove to wire racks; cool completely.

Makes 3 dozen cookies

Tip: For a fun flavor adventure, fill ravioli cookies with 1-inch squares of semisweet or milk chocolate instead of brown sugar-pecan mixture. Omit steps 1 and 2.

Pecan Toffee Filled Ravioli Cookies

Chocolate Almond Biscotti

3 cups all-purpose flour
½ cup unsweetened cocoa
2 teaspoons baking powder
½ teaspoon salt
1 cup granulated sugar
⅔ cup margarine, softened
¾ cup EGG BEATERS® Healthy Real Egg
    Substitute
1 teaspoon almond extract
½ cup whole blanched almonds, toasted and
    coarsely chopped
    Powdered Sugar Glaze (recipe follows)

In medium bowl, combine flour, cocoa, baking powder and salt; set aside.

In large bowl, with electric mixer at medium speed, beat granulated sugar and margarine for 2 minutes or until creamy. Add Egg Beaters® and almond extract; beat well. With electric mixer at low speed, gradually add flour mixture, beating just until blended; stir in almonds.

On lightly greased baking sheet, form dough into two (12×2½-inch) logs. Bake at 350°F for 25 to 30 minutes or until toothpick inserted in centers comes out clean. Remove from sheet; cool on wire racks 15 minutes.

Using serrated knife, slice each log diagonally into 12 (1-inch-thick) slices; place, cut-sides up, on same baking sheet. Bake at 350°F for 12 to 15 minutes on each side or until cookies are crisp and edges are browned. Remove from sheet; cool completely on wire rack. Drizzle tops with Powdered Sugar Glaze.   *Makes 2 dozen cookies*

Powdered Sugar Glaze: In small bowl, combine 1 cup powdered sugar and 5 to 6 teaspoons water until smooth.

Nutrients per Serving (1 cookie):

Calories: 160, Total Fat: 7 g, Cholesterol: 0 mg, Sodium: 125 mg

Cocoa Kiss Cookies

1 cup (2 sticks) butter or margarine,
    softened
⅔ cup sugar
1 teaspoon vanilla extract
1⅔ cups all-purpose flour
¼ cup HERSHEY'S Cocoa
1 cup finely chopped pecans
1 bag (9 ounces) HERSHEY'S KISSES
    Milk Chocolates
    Powdered sugar

Beat butter, sugar and vanilla in large bowl until creamy. Stir together flour and cocoa; gradually add to butter mixture, beating until blended. Add pecans; beat until well blended. Refrigerate dough about 1 hour or until firm enough to handle. Heat oven to 375°F. Remove wrappers from chocolate pieces. Mold scant tablespoon of dough around each chocolate piece, covering completely. Shape into balls. Place on ungreased cookie sheet. Bake 10 to 12 minutes or until set. Cool slightly, about 1 minute; remove from cookie sheet to wire rack. Cool completely. Roll in powdered sugar. Roll in sugar again just before serving, if desired.

Makes about 4½ dozen cookies

Chocolate Almond Biscotti

Spiced Chocolate Pecan Squares

COOKIE BASE

1 cup all-purpose flour
½ cup packed light brown sugar
½ teaspoon baking soda
¼ cup (½ stick) butter or margarine, softened

TOPPING

1 package (8 ounces) semi-sweet chocolate baking squares
2 large eggs
¼ cup packed light brown sugar
¼ cup light corn syrup
2 tablespoons FRENCH'S® Worcestershire Sauce
1 tablespoon vanilla extract
1½ cups chopped pecans or walnuts, divided

Preheat oven to 375°F. To prepare cookie base, place flour, ½ cup sugar and baking soda in food processor or bowl of electric mixer. Process or mix 10 seconds. Add butter. Process or beat 30 seconds or until mixture resembles fine crumbs. Press evenly into bottom of greased 9-inch baking pan. Bake 15 minutes.

Meanwhile, to prepare topping, place chocolate in microwave-safe bowl. Microwave, uncovered, on HIGH (100%) power 2 minutes or until chocolate is melted, stirring until chocolate is smooth; set aside.

Place eggs, ¼ cup sugar, corn syrup, Worcestershire and vanilla in food processor or bowl of electric mixer. Process or beat until well blended. Add melted chocolate. Process or beat

until smooth. Stir in 1 cup nuts. Pour chocolate mixture over cookie base. Sprinkle with remaining ½ cup nuts. Bake 40 minutes or until toothpick inserted into center comes out with slightly fudgy crumbs. (Cookie will be slightly puffed.) Cool completely on wire rack. To serve, cut into squares.   *Makes 16 servings*

Chocolate-Dipped Oat Cookies

2 cups uncooked old-fashioned or quick oats
¾ cup firmly packed brown sugar
½ cup vegetable oil
½ cup finely chopped walnuts
1 egg
2 teaspoons grated orange peel
¼ teaspoon salt
1 package (12 ounces) milk chocolate chips

Combine oats, sugar, oil, walnuts, egg, orange peel and salt in large bowl until blended. Cover; refrigerate overnight.

Preheat oven to 350°F. Lightly grease cookie sheets or line with parchment paper. Shape oat mixture into large marble-sized balls. Place 2 inches apart on prepared cookie sheets.

Bake 10 to 12 minutes or until golden and crisp. Cool 10 minutes on wire racks. Meanwhile, melt chocolate chips in top of double boiler over hot (not boiling) water; keep warm. Dip tops of cookies, one at a time, into melted chocolate. Place on waxed paper; cool until chocolate is set.
Makes about 6 dozen cookies

Spiced Chocolate Pecan Squares

Spicy Lemon Crescents

   1 cup (2 sticks) butter or margarine,
      softened
1½ cups powdered sugar, divided
   ½ teaspoon lemon extract
   ½ teaspoon grated lemon zest
   2 cups cake flour
   ½ cup finely chopped almonds, walnuts or
      pecans
   1 teaspoon ground cinnamon
   ½ teaspoon ground cardamom
   ½ teaspoon ground nutmeg
1¾ cups "M&M's"® Chocolate Mini Baking
      Bits

Preheat oven to 375°F. Lightly grease cookie
sheets; set aside. In large bowl cream butter and
½ cup sugar; add lemon extract and zest until
well blended. In medium bowl combine flour,
nuts, cinnamon, cardamom and nutmeg; add to
creamed mixture until well blended. Stir in
"M&M's"® Chocolate Mini Baking Bits. Using
1 tablespoon of dough at a time, form into
crescent shapes; place about 2 inches apart on
prepared cookie sheets. Bake 12 to 14 minutes or
until edges are golden. Cool 2 minutes on cookie
sheets. Gently roll warm crescents in remaining
1 cup sugar. Cool completely on wire racks. Store
in tightly covered container.

Makes about 2 dozen cookies

Chocolate Cherry Cookies

   2 squares (1 ounce *each*) unsweetened
      chocolate
   ½ cup butter, softened
   ½ cup sugar
   1 egg
   2 cups cake flour
   1 teaspoon vanilla
   ¼ teaspoon salt
      Maraschino cherries, well drained
      (about 48)
   1 cup (6 ounces) semisweet or milk
      chocolate chips

Melt unsweetened chocolate in top of double
boiler over hot, not boiling, water. Remove from
heat; cool. Beat butter and sugar in large bowl
until light. Add egg and melted chocolate; beat
until fluffy. Stir in cake flour, vanilla and salt
until well blended. Cover; refrigerate until firm,
about 1 hour.

Preheat oven to 400°F. Lightly grease cookie
sheets or line with parchment paper. Shape
dough into 1-inch balls. Place 2 inches apart on
prepared cookie sheets. With knuckle of finger,
make deep indentation in center of each ball.
Place cherry into each indentation. Bake
8 minutes or just until set. Meanwhile, melt
chocolate chips in small bowl over hot water. Stir
until melted. Remove cookies to wire racks.
Drizzle melted chocolate over tops of cookies
while still warm. Refrigerate until chocolate
is set.   *Makes about 4 dozen cookies*

Spicy Lemon Crescents

Heavenly HOLIDAY CREATIONS

Valentine Stained Glass Hearts

   ½ **cup butter or margarine, softened**
   ¾ **cup granulated sugar**
   2 **eggs**
   1 **teaspoon vanilla extract**
2⅓ **cups all-purpose flour**
   1 **teaspoon baking powder**
     Red hard candies, crushed (about ⅓ cup)
     Frosting (optional)

Cream butter and sugar in mixing bowl. Beat in eggs and vanilla. Sift flour and baking powder together. Gradually stir in flour mixture until dough is very stiff. Cover and chill 3 hours to overnight.

Preheat oven to 375°F. Roll out dough to ⅛-inch thickness on lightly floured surface. To prevent cookies from becoming tough and brittle, do not incorporate too much flour. Cut out cookies using large heart-shaped cookie cutter or use sharp knife and cut heart design. Transfer cookies to foil-lined baking sheet. Using small heart-shaped cookie cutter, cut out and remove heart design from center of each cookie. Fill cutout sections with crushed candy. Bake 7 to 9 minutes or until cookies are lightly browned and candy has melted. *Do not overbake.*

Remove from oven; immediately slide foil off baking sheet. Cool completely; carefully loosen cookies from foil. If desired, pipe decorative borders with frosting around edges.
     Makes about 2½ dozen medium cookies

Favorite recipe from **The Sugar Association, Inc.**

Valentine Stained Glass Hearts

Festive Easter Cookies

1 cup butter, softened
2 cups powdered sugar
1 egg
2 teaspoons grated lemon peel
1 teaspoon vanilla
3 cups all-purpose flour
½ teaspoon salt
    Royal Icing (recipe follows)
    Assorted food colors, icings and candies

1. Beat butter and sugar in large bowl at high speed of electric mixer until fluffy. Add egg, lemon peel and vanilla; mix well. Combine flour and salt in medium bowl. Add to butter mixture; mix well. Divide dough into 2 sections. Cover with plastic wrap. Refrigerate 3 hours or overnight.

2. Preheat oven to 375°F. Roll dough on floured surface to ⅛-inch thickness. Cut out cookies using Easter cookie cutters, such as eggs, bunnies and tulips. Place on ungreased cookie sheets.

3. Bake 8 to 12 minutes or just until edges are very lightly browned. Remove to wire racks; cool completely. Prepare Royal Icing. Decorate as desired. Let stand until icing is set.

Makes 4 dozen cookies

Royal Icing

1 egg white, at room temperature
2 to 2½ cups sifted powdered sugar
½ teaspoon almond extract

Beat egg white in bowl at high speed of electric mixer until foamy. Gradually add 2 cups powdered sugar and almond extract; beat until moistened. Increase speed to high; beat until icing is stiff.

Cocoa Almond Cut-Out Cookies

¾ cup (1½ sticks) margarine, softened
1 (14-ounce) can sweetened condensed milk (NOT evaporated milk)
2 eggs
1 teaspoon vanilla extract
½ teaspoon almond extract
2¾ cups all-purpose flour
⅔ cup HERSHEY'S Cocoa
2 teaspoons baking powder
½ teaspoon baking soda
½ cup finely chopped almonds
    Chocolate Glaze (recipe follows)

Beat margarine, sweetened condensed milk, eggs and extracts in large bowl until well blended. Stir together flour, cocoa, baking powder and baking soda; add to margarine mixture. Beat until blended. Stir in almonds. Divide dough into 4 equal portions. Wrap in plastic wrap; flatten. Chill until firm enough to roll, about 2 hours.

Heat oven to 350°F. Lightly grease cookie sheet. Working with 1 portion at a time (keep remaining dough in refrigerator), on floured surface, roll to about ⅛-inch thickness. Cut into desired shapes. Place on prepared cookie sheets. Bake 6 to 8 minutes or until set. Remove from cookie sheet to wire racks; cool completely. Drizzle with Chocolate Glaze. Store tightly covered at room temperature.

Makes about 6 dozen (3-inch) cookies

Chocolate Glaze: Melt 1 cup (6 ounces) HERSHEY'S Semi-Sweet Chocolate Chips with 2 tablespoons shortening. Makes about ⅔ cup.

Festive Easter Cookies

Greeting Card Cookies

½ cup (1 stick) butter or margarine, softened
¾ cup sugar
1 egg
1 teaspoon vanilla extract
1½ cups all-purpose flour
⅓ cup HERSHEY'S Cocoa
½ teaspoon baking powder
½ teaspoon baking soda
¼ teaspoon salt
Decorative Frosting (recipe follows)

Beat butter, sugar, egg and vanilla in large bowl until light and fluffy. Stir together flour, cocoa, baking powder, baking soda and salt; add to butter mixture, blending well. Refrigerate about 1 hour or until firm enough to roll. Cut cardboard rectangle for pattern, 2½×4 inches; wrap in plastic wrap.

Preheat oven to 350°F. On lightly floured board or between two pieces of waxed paper, roll out half of dough to ¼-inch thickness. Place pattern on dough; cut through dough around pattern with sharp paring knife. (Save dough trimmings and reroll for remaining cookies.) Carefully place cutouts on lightly greased cookie sheet; bake 8 to 10 minutes or until set. Cool 1 minute on cookie sheet. (If cookies have lost their shape, trim irregular edges while cookies are still hot.) Carefully transfer to cooling rack. Repeat procedure with remaining dough. Prepare Decorative Frosting; spoon into pastry bag fitted with decorating tip. Pipe names or greetings onto cookies; decorate as desired.

Makes about 12 cookies

Decorative Frosting

3 cups powdered sugar
⅓ cup shortening
2 to 3 tablespoons milk
Food color (optional)

In small bowl, beat sugar and shortening; gradually add milk, beating until smooth and slightly thickened. Divide frosting into two bowls; tint with food color, if desired. Cover until ready to use.

Pumpkin Jingle Bars

1 two-layer spice cake mix
1 (16-ounce) can pumpkin
¾ cup MIRACLE WHIP® Salad Dressing
3 eggs
Sifted confectioners' sugar
Vanilla frosting
Red and green gum drops, sliced

Mix first 4 ingredients in large bowl at medium speed of electric mixer until well blended. Pour into greased 15½×10½×1-inch jelly roll pan. Bake at 350°F 18 to 20 minutes or until edges pull away from sides of pan. Cool. Sprinkle with sugar. Cut into bars. Decorate with frosting and gum drops. *Makes about 3 dozen bars*

Prep Time: 5 minutes
Cook Time: 20 minutes

Candy Corn Cookies

¾ **cup butter, softened**
¼ **cup granulated sugar**
¼ **cup packed light brown sugar**
1 **egg yolk**
1¾ **cups all-purpose flour**
¾ **teaspoon baking powder**
⅛ **teaspoon salt**
   Cookie Glaze (recipe follows)
   Yellow and orange food colors

1. Combine butter, sugars and egg yolk in meduim bowl. Add flour, baking powder and salt; mix well. Cover; refrigerate about 4 hours or until firm.

2. Preheat oven to 350°F.

3. Roll dough on floured surface to ¼-inch thickness. Cut out candy corn shapes from dough. Place cutouts on ungreased cookie sheets.

4. Bake 8 to 10 minutes or until edges are lightly browned. Remove to wire racks to cool.

5. Prepare Cookie Glaze. Place racks over waxed-paper-covered baking sheets. Divide cookie glaze into thirds; place in separate small bowls. Color ⅓ of glaze with yellow food color and ⅓ with orange food color. Leave remaining glaze white. Spoon different colored glazes over cookies to resemble "candy corn" as shown in photo. Let stand until glaze is set.

Makes about 2 dozen cookies

Cookie Glaze

4 **cups powdered sugar**
4 **to 6 tablespoons milk**

Combine powdered sugar and enough milk, one tablespoon at a time, to make a medium-thick pourable glaze.

Bat Cookies: Omit yellow and orange food colors. Prepare recipe as directed except cut out bat shapes. Bake as directed. Color glaze with black paste food color; spoon over cookies. Decorate with assorted candies as shown in photo.

Old-Fashioned Molasses Cookies

4 **cups sifted all-purpose flour**
2 **teaspoons ARM & HAMMER® Pure Baking Soda**
1½ **teaspoons ground ginger**
½ **teaspoon ground cinnamon**
⅛ **teaspoon salt**
1½ **cups molasses**
½ **cup shortening, melted**
¼ **cup butter or margarine, melted**
⅓ **cup boiling water**
   Sugar

In medium bowl, combine flour, baking soda, spices and salt. In large bowl, mix molasses, shortening, butter and water. Add dry ingredients to molasses mixture; blend well. Cover; refrigerate until firm, about 2 hours. Roll out dough ¼ inch thick on well-floured surface. Cut out with 3½-inch cookie cutters; sprinkle with sugar. Place 2 inches apart on ungreased cookie sheets. Bake in preheated 375°F oven about 12 minutes. Remove to wire racks to cool.

Makes about 3 dozen cookies

Top to bottom: Bat Cookies and Candy Corn Cookies

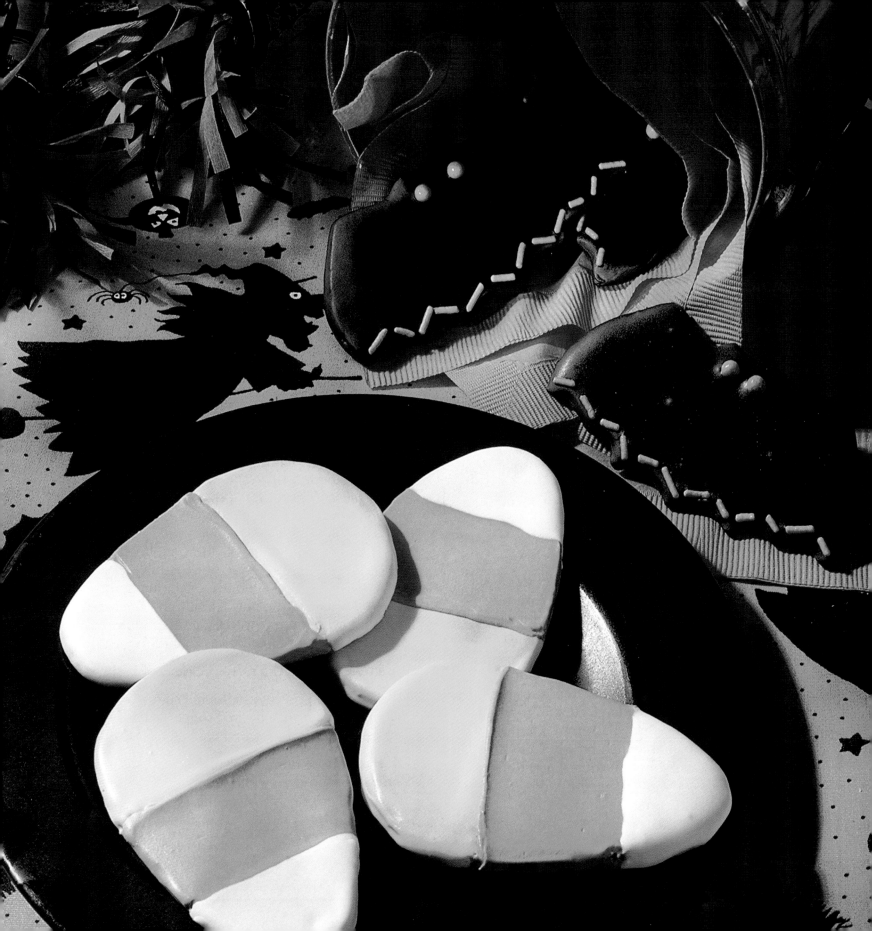

Star Christmas Tree Cookies

COOKIES

½ CRISCO® Stick or ½ cup CRISCO® all-vegetable shortening
⅓ cup butter or margarine, softened
2 egg yolks
1 teaspoon vanilla extract
1 package DUNCAN HINES® Moist Deluxe Yellow or Devil's Food Cake Mix
1 tablespoon water, divided

FROSTING

1 container (16 ounces) DUNCAN HINES® Creamy Homestyle Vanilla Frosting
Green food coloring
Red and green sugar crystals for garnish
Assorted colored candies and decors for garnish

Preheat oven to 375°F.

For Cookies, combine shortening, butter, egg yolks and vanilla extract. Blend in cake mix gradually. Add 1 teaspoonful water at a time until dough is rolling consistency. Divide dough into 4 balls. Flatten one ball with hand; roll to ⅛-inch thickness on lightly floured surface. Cut with graduated star cookie cutters. Repeat using remaining dough. Bake large cookies together on ungreased baking sheet. Bake 6 to 8 minutes or until edges are light golden brown. Cool cookies 1 minute. Remove from baking sheet. Repeat with smaller cookies, testing for doneness at minimum baking time.

For Frosting, tint vanilla frosting with green food coloring. Frost cookies and stack beginning with largest cookies on bottom and ending with smallest cookies on top. Rotate cookies when stacking to alternate corners. Decorate as desired with colored sugar crystals and assorted colored candies and decors.   *Makes 2 to 3 dozen cookies*

Gingerbread Cookies

½ cup shortening
⅓ cup packed light brown sugar
¼ cup dark molasses
1 egg white
½ teaspoon vanilla
1½ cups all-purpose flour
½ teaspoon baking soda
¼ teaspoon baking powder
½ teaspoon salt
1 teaspoon ground cinnamon
½ teaspoon ground ginger

1. Beat shortening, brown sugar, molasses, egg white and vanilla in large bowl at high speed of electric mixer until smooth. Combine flour, baking soda, baking powder, salt and spices in small bowl. Add to shortening mixture; mix well. Cover; refrigerate until firm, about 8 hours.

2. Preheat oven to 350°F. Grease cookie sheets.

3. Roll dough on lightly floured surface to ⅛-inch thickness. Cut into desired shapes with cookie cutters. Place on prepared cookie sheets.

4. Bake 6 to 8 minutes or until edges begin to brown. Remove to wire racks; cool completely.
Makes about 2½ dozen cookies

Star Christmas Tree Cookies

Fried Norwegian Cookies

2 eggs, at room temperature
3 tablespoons granulated sugar
¼ cup butter, melted
2 tablespoons milk
1 teaspoon vanilla
1½ to 2 cups all-purpose flour
Vegetable oil
Powdered sugar

Beat eggs and sugar in large bowl with electric mixer at medium speed until thick and lemon colored. Beat in butter, milk and vanilla until well blended. Gradually add 1½ cups flour. Beat at low speed until well blended. Stir in enough remaining flour with spoon to form soft dough. Divide dough into 4 portions; cover and refrigerate until firm, at least 2 hours or overnight.

Working with floured hands, shape 1 portion dough at a time into 1-inch-thick square. Place dough on lightly floured surface. Roll out dough to 11-inch square. Cut dough into 1¼-inch strips; cut strips diagonally at 2-inch intervals. Cut 1¼-inch slit vertically down center of each strip. Insert one end of strip through cut to form twist; repeat with each strip. Repeat with remaining dough.

Heat oil in large saucepan to 365°F. Place 12 cookies at a time in hot oil. Fry about 1½ minutes or until golden brown, turning cookies once with slotted spoon. Drain on paper towels. Dust cookies with powdered sugar. Cookies are best if served immediately, but can be stored in airtight container 1 day.

Makes about 11 dozen cookies

Cinnamon Crinkles Cookies

TOPPINGS
2 tablespoons sugar
½ teaspoon ground cinnamon
2 egg whites
1 teaspoon water

COOKIES
¾ cup butter or margarine, softened
2 egg yolks
1 teaspoon vanilla extract
1 package DUNCAN HINES® Moist Deluxe French Vanilla Flavor Cake Mix
48 whole almonds or pecan halves for garnish (optional)

1. Preheat oven to 375°F.

2. For Toppings, combine sugar and cinnamon in small bowl; set aside. Combine egg whites and water in another small bowl; beat lightly with fork. Set aside.

3. For Cookies, combine butter, egg yolks and vanilla extract in large bowl. Blend in cake mix gradually. Stir until thoroughly blended. Roll 1 level measuring teaspoon dough into ball. Dip half the ball into egg white mixture then into cinnamon-sugar mixture. Place ball sugar-side-up on ungreased baking sheet. Press nut on top. Repeat with remaining dough placing balls 2 inches apart. Bake at 375°F for 9 to 10 minutes or until puffed and edges are light golden brown. Cool 2 minutes on baking sheets. Remove to cooling rack. Store in airtight container.

Makes 48 cookies

Fried Norwegian Cookies

Apple Sauce Gingerbread Cookies

4 cups all-purpose flour
2 teaspoons ground ginger
2 teaspoons ground cinnamon
1 teaspoon baking soda
½ teaspoon salt
¼ teaspoon ground nutmeg
½ cup margarine, softened
1 cup sugar
⅓ cup light molasses
1 cup MOTT'S® Natural Apple Sauce
Decorator Icing (recipe follows)

Sift together flour, ginger, cinnamon, baking soda, salt and nutmeg; set aside. In bowl, with electric mixer at high speed, beat margarine, sugar and molasses until creamy. Alternately blend in dry ingredients and apple sauce. Cover and chill dough for several hours or overnight.

Preheat oven to 375°F. On floured surface, roll dough out to ⅛-inch thickness with lightly floured rolling pin. Cut with floured gingerbread man cutter or other shapes. Place on greased baking sheet. Bake 12 minutes or until done. Remove from sheet; cool on wire rack. Frost with Decorator Icing as desired. After icing dries, store in airtight container.

Makes 2½ dozen (5½-inch) cookies

Decorator Icing: Mix 2 cups confectioners' sugar and 1 tablespoon water. Add more water, 1 teaspoon at a time, until icing holds its shape and can be piped through decorating tube.

Chocolate Spritz Cookies

1 package DUNCAN HINES® Golden
Sugar Cookie Mix
⅓ cup unsweetened cocoa
1 egg
⅓ cup CRISCO® Oil or CRISCO®
PURITAN® Canola Oil
2 tablespoons water

1. Preheat oven to 375°F.

2. Combine cookie mix and cocoa in large mixing bowl. Stir until blended. Add egg, oil and water. Stir until thoroughly blended.

3. Fill cookie press with dough. Press desired shapes 2 inches apart onto ungreased cookie sheets. Bake at 375°F for 6 to 8 minutes or until set. Cool 1 minute on baking sheets. Remove to cooling racks. Cool completely.

Makes 5 to 6 dozen cookies

Note: For a delicious no-cholesterol variation, substitute 2 egg whites for whole egg.

Tip: For festive cookies, decorate before baking with assorted decors or after baking with melted milk, semi-sweet or white chocolate and chopped nuts.

Chocolate Spritz Cookies

Linzer Sandwich Cookies

1⅓ cups all-purpose flour
¼ teaspoon baking powder
¼ teaspoon salt
¾ cup granulated sugar
½ cup butter, softened
1 egg
1 teaspoon vanilla
   Powdered sugar (optional)
   Seedless raspberry jam

Combine flour, baking powder and salt in small bowl. Beat granulated sugar and butter in medium bowl with electric mixer at medium speed until light and fluffy. Beat in egg and vanilla. Gradually add flour mixture. Beat at low speed until dough forms. Divide dough in half; cover and refrigerate 2 hours or until firm.

Preheat oven to 375°F. Working with 1 portion at a time, roll out dough on lightly floured surface to ⅛-inch thickness. Cut dough into desired shapes with floured cookie cutters. Cut out equal numbers of each shape. (If dough becomes too soft, refrigerate several minutes before continuing.) Cut 1-inch centers out of half the cookies of each shape. Reroll trimmings and cut out more cookies. Place cookies 1½ to 2 inches apart on ungreased cookie sheets. Bake 7 to 9 minutes or until edges are lightly brown. Let cookies stand on cookie sheets 1 to 2 minutes. Remove cookies to wire racks; cool completely.

Sprinkle cookies that have holes with powdered sugar, if desired. Spread 1 teaspoon jam on flat side of whole cookies, spreading almost to edges. Place cookies with holes, flat side down, over jam.   *Makes about 2 dozen cookies*

Santa's Chocolate Cookies

1 cup butter
⅔ cup semisweet chocolate chips
¾ cup sugar
1 egg
½ teaspoon vanilla
2 cups all-purpose flour
   Apricot jam, melted semisweet chocolate, chopped almonds, frosting, coconut or colored sprinkles

Preheat oven to 350°F. Melt butter and chocolate chips together in small saucepan over low heat or microwave for 2 minutes at HIGH (100%) power until completely melted. Combine chocolate mixture and sugar in large bowl. Add egg and vanilla; stir well. Add flour; stir well. Refrigerate 30 minutes or until firm.

Shape dough into 1-inch balls. Place 1 inch apart on ungreased cookie sheets. If desired, flatten balls with bottom of drinking glass, shape into logs or make a depression in center and fill with apricot jam.

Bake 8 to 10 minutes or until set. Remove to wire racks to cool completely. Decorate as desired with melted chocolate, almonds, frosting, coconut and colored sprinkles.

Makes about 3 dozen cookies

Linzer Sandwich Cookies

Chocolate Thumbprint Cookies

½ cup (1 stick) butter or margarine, softened
⅔ cup sugar
1 egg, separated
2 tablespoons milk
1 teaspoon vanilla extract
1 cup all-purpose flour
⅓ cup HERSHEY'S Cocoa
¼ teaspoon salt
1 cup chopped nuts
Vanilla Filling (recipe follows)
26 HERSHEY'S KISSES Milk Chocolates or
HERSHEY'S HUGS Chocolates or
pecan halves or candied cherry halves

Beat butter, sugar, egg yolk, milk and vanilla in small mixer bowl until light and fluffy. Stir together flour, cocoa and salt; gradually add to butter mixture, beating until blended. Cover; refrigerate dough at least 1 hour or until firm enough to handle. Heat oven to 350°F. Lightly grease cookie sheet. Shape dough into 1-inch balls. With fork, beat egg white slightly. Dip each ball into egg white; roll in nuts. Place on prepared cookie sheet. Press thumb gently in center of each cookie.

Bake cookies 10 to 12 minutes or until set. Meanwhile, prepare Vanilla Filling. Remove wrappers from chocolate pieces. Remove cookies from cookie sheet to wire rack; cool 5 minutes. Spoon about ¼ teaspoon prepared filling into each thumbprint. Gently press chocolate piece onto top of each cookie. Cool completely.
Makes about 2 dozen cookies

Vanilla Filling

½ cup powdered sugar
1 tablespoon butter or margarine, softened
2 teaspoons milk
¼ teaspoon vanilla extract

In small bowl, combine powdered sugar, butter, milk and vanilla; beat until smooth.

Snow Covered Almond Crescents

1 cup (2 sticks) margarine or butter, softened
¾ cup powdered sugar
½ teaspoon almond extract or 2 teaspoons vanilla
1¾ cups all-purpose flour
¼ teaspoon salt (optional)
1 cup QUAKER® Oats (quick or old fashioned, uncooked)
½ cup finely chopped almonds
Powdered sugar

Preheat oven to 325°F. Beat margarine, sugar and almond extract until well blended. Add flour and salt, if desired; mix until well blended. Stir in oats and almonds. Using level measuring tablespoonfuls, shape dough into crescents. Bake on ungreased cookie sheet 14 to 17 minutes or until bottoms are light golden brown. Remove to wire rack. Sift additional powdered sugar generously over warm cookies. Cool completely. Store tightly covered.
Makes about 3 dozen cookies

Snow Covered Almond Crescents

Christmas Ornament Cookies

2¼ cups all-purpose flour
¼ teaspoon salt
1 cup granulated sugar
¾ cup butter, softened
1 egg
1 teaspoon vanilla
1 teaspoon almond extract
Icing (recipe follows)
Assorted candies or decors

Combine flour and salt in medium bowl. Beat sugar and butter in large bowl with electric mixer at medium speed until light and fluffy. Beat in egg, vanilla and almond extract. Gradually add flour mixture. Beat at low speed until well blended. Divide dough in half; cover and refrigerate 30 minutes or until firm.

Preheat oven to 350°F. Working with 1 portion at a time, roll out dough on lightly floured surface to ¼-inch thickness. Cut dough into desired shapes with assorted floured cookie cutters. Reroll trimmings and cut out more cookies. Place cutouts on ungreased cookie sheets. Using drinking straw or tip of sharp knife, cut a hole near top of each cookie to allow for piece of ribbon or string to be inserted for hanger. Bake 10 to 12 minutes or until edges are golden brown. Let cookies stand on cookie sheets 1 minute. Remove cookies to wire racks; cool completely.

Prepare Icing. Spoon Icing into small resealable plastic food storage bag. Cut off very tiny corner of bag; pipe Icing decoratively over cookies. Decorate with candies as desired. Let stand at room temperature 40 minutes or until set. Thread ribbon through each cookie hole to hang as Christmas tree ornaments.

Makes about 2 dozen cookies

Icing

2 cups powdered sugar
2 tablespoons milk or lemon juice
Food coloring (optional)

Place powdered sugar and milk in small bowl; stir with spoon until smooth. (Icing will be very thick. If it is too thick, stir in 1 teaspoon additional milk.) Divide into small bowls and tint with food coloring, if desired.

Christmas Spritz Cookies

2¼ cups all-purpose flour
¼ teaspoon salt
1¼ cups powdered sugar
1 cup butter, softened
1 egg
1 teaspoon vanilla
1 teaspoon almond extract
　Green food coloring (optional)
　Candied red and green cherries and
　　assorted decorative candies (optional)
　Icing (recipe follows, optional)

Preheat oven to 375°F. Combine flour and salt in medium bowl. Beat powdered sugar and butter in large bowl with electric mixer until light and fluffy. Beat in egg, vanilla and almond extract. Gradually add flour mixture. Beat at low speed until well blended.

Divide dough in half. If desired, tint half of dough green with food coloring. Fit cookie press with desired plate (or change plates for different shapes after first batch). Fill press with dough; press dough 1 inch apart onto ungreased cookie sheets. Decorate cookies with cherries and assorted candies, if desired.

Bake 10 to 12 minutes or until just set. Remove cookies to wire racks; cool completely.

Prepare Icing, if desired. Pipe or drizzle on cooled cookies. Decorate with cherries and assorted candies, if desired.　　*Makes about 5 dozen cookies*

Icing

1½ cups powdered sugar
2 tablespoons milk plus additional, if needed
⅛ teaspoon almond extract

Place powdered sugar, milk and almond extract in medium bowl; stir with spoon until smooth.

Chocolate Crinkle Cookies

2 cups granulated sugar
¾ cup vegetable oil
¾ cup HERSHEY'S Cocoa
4 eggs
2 teaspoons vanilla extract
2⅓ cups all-purpose flour
2 teaspoons baking powder
½ teaspoon salt
　Powdered sugar

Stir together granulated sugar and oil; add cocoa, blending well. Beat in eggs and vanilla. In separate bowl, stir together flour, baking powder and salt; add to cocoa mixture, blending well. Cover; refrigerate at least 6 hours.

Heat oven to 350°F. Grease cookie sheet. Shape dough into 1-inch balls; roll in powdered sugar. Place 2 inches apart on prepared cookie sheet. Bake 12 to 14 minutes or until almost no indentation remains when touched. Remove from cookie sheet to wire rack. Cool completely.
　　Makes about 4 dozen cookies

Christmas Spritz Cookies

Spicy Gingerbread Cookies

COOKIES

¾ cup (1½ sticks) butter, softened
⅔ cup light molasses
½ cup firmly packed brown sugar
1 egg
1½ teaspoons grated lemon peel
2½ cups all-purpose flour
1¼ teaspoons ground cinnamon
1 teaspoon ground allspice
1 teaspoon vanilla
½ teaspoon baking soda
½ teaspoon salt
½ teaspoon ground ginger
¼ teaspoon baking powder

FROSTING

4 cups powdered sugar
½ cup (1 stick) butter, softened
4 tablespoons milk
2 teaspoons vanilla
Food coloring (optional)

For Cookies, combine butter, molasses, brown sugar, egg and lemon peel in large bowl. Beat at medium speed until smooth and creamy. Add all remaining cookie ingredients. Reduce speed to low; beat well. Cover; refrigerate at least 2 hours.

Preheat oven to 350°F. Roll out dough, one half at a time, on well floured surface to ¼-inch thickness. (Keeping remaining dough refrigerated.) Cut with 3- to 4-inch cookie cutters. Place on greased cookie sheets. Bake 6 to 8 minutes or until no indentation remains when touched. Remove immediately. Cool completely.

For Frosting, combine powdered sugar, butter, milk and vanilla in small bowl. Beat at low speed until fluffy. Color frosting with food coloring, if desired. Decorate cookies with frosting.

Makes about 4 dozen cookies

Soft Spicy Molasses Cookies

2 cups all-purpose flour
1 cup sugar
¾ cup butter, softened
⅓ cup light molasses
3 tablespoons milk
1 egg
½ teaspoon baking soda
½ teaspoon ground ginger
½ teaspoon ground cinnamon
½ teaspoon ground cloves
⅛ teaspoon salt
Additional sugar for rolling

Combine flour, 1 cup sugar, butter, molasses, milk, egg, baking soda, ginger, cinnamon, cloves and salt in large bowl. Beat at low speed of electric mixer until well blended, 2 to 3 minutes. Cover; refrigerate until firm enough to handle, at least 4 hours or overnight.

Preheat oven to 350°F. Shape rounded teaspoonfuls of dough into 1-inch balls. Roll in sugar. Place 2 inches apart on ungreased cookie sheets. Bake 10 to 12 minutes or until slightly firm to the touch. Remove immediately.

Makes about 4 dozen cookies

Spicy Gingerbread Cookies

Chocolate-Topped Linzer Cookies

3 cups hazelnuts, toasted, skins removed, divided
1 cup unsalted butter, softened
1 cup powdered sugar, sifted
½ teaspoon grated lemon peel
¼ teaspoon salt
½ egg*
3 cups sifted all-purpose flour
½ cup nougat paste**
½ cup seedless red raspberry jam
6 squares (1 ounce *each*) semisweet chocolate
2 tablespoons shortening

*To measure ½ egg, lightly beat 1 egg in glass measuring cup; remove half for use in recipe.

**Nougat paste, a mixture of ground hazelnuts, sugar and semisweet chocolate is available in specialty candy and gourmet food shops. If unavailable, substitute melted semisweet chocolate to attach cookie layers.

Place 1½ cups hazelnuts in food processor or blender; process until finely ground. (You should have ½ cup ground nuts; if necessary, process more nuts.) Set aside remaining whole nuts for garnish.

Beat butter, sugar, lemon peel and salt in large bowl until thoroughly blended. *Do not overmix.* Add ½ egg; beat until well mixed. Stir in ground hazelnuts. Gradually stir in flour. Divide dough into quarters. Wrap each portion; refrigerate until firm, about 2 hours.

Preheat oven to 350°F. Line cookie sheets with parchment paper. Roll out dough, one quarter at a time, ⅛ inch thick on floured pastry cloth. Cut out with 1¼-inch round cutter. Place ¾ inch apart on prepared cookie sheets.

Bake 7 to 8 minutes or until lightly browned. Cool completely on cookie sheets set on wire racks. Spoon nougat paste into pastry bag fitted with ¼-inch round tip. Pipe about ¼ teaspoon paste onto centers of ⅓ of cookies. Top with plain cookies; press gently.

Spoon raspberry jam into pastry bag fitted with ⅓-inch round tip. Pipe about ⅓ teaspoon jam onto centers of second cookie layers. Top with plain cookies; press gently. Let cookies stand about 1 hour.

Melt chocolate and shortening in small, heavy saucepan over low heat; stir until smooth. Press cookie layers lightly together. Dip top of each cookie into chocolate mixture just to cover. Shake to remove excess chocolate. Place cookies, chocolate-side-up, on wire racks; press reserved whole hazelnuts into soft chocolate in centers of cookies. Let stand until chocolate is set.

Makes about 4 dozen cookies

ACKNOWLEDGMENTS

The publisher would like to thank the companies and organizations listed below for the use of their recipes and photographs in this publication.

Arm & Hammer Division, Church & Dwight Co., Inc.

Best Foods

Blue Diamond Growers®

Cherry Marketing Institute, Inc.

Dole Food Company, Inc.

Egg Beaters® Healthy Real Egg Substitute

Hershey Foods Corporation

The J.M. Smucker Company

Kellogg Company

Kraft Foods, Inc.

M&M/MARS

MOTT'S® Inc., a division of Cadbury Beverages Inc.

Nabisco Biscuit Company

Nestlé USA, Inc.

The Procter & Gamble Company

The Quaker® Kitchens

Reckitt & Colman Inc.

Sokol & Company

The Sugar Association, Inc.

Washington Apple Commission

INDEX

METRIC CONVERSION CHART

VOLUME MEASUREMENTS (dry)

⅛ teaspoon = 0.5 mL
¼ teaspoon = 1 mL
½ teaspoon = 2 mL
¾ teaspoon = 4 mL
1 teaspoon = 5 mL
1 tablespoon = 15 mL
2 tablespoons = 30 mL
¼ cup = 60 mL
⅓ cup = 75 mL
½ cup = 125 mL
⅔ cup = 150 mL
¾ cup = 175 mL
1 cup = 250 mL
2 cups = 1 pint = 500 mL
3 cups = 750 mL
4 cups = 1 quart = 1 L

VOLUME MEASUREMENTS (fluid)

1 fluid ounce (2 tablespoons) = 30 mL
4 fluid ounces (½ cup) = 125 mL
8 fluid ounces (1 cup) = 250 mL
12 fluid ounces (1½ cups) = 375 mL
16 fluid ounces (2 cups) = 500 mL

WEIGHTS (mass)

½ ounce = 15 g
1 ounce = 30 g
3 ounces = 90 g
4 ounces = 120 g
8 ounces = 225 g
10 ounces = 285 g
12 ounces = 360 g
16 ounces = 1 pound = 450 g

DIMENSIONS

$\frac{1}{16}$ inch = 2 mm
⅛ inch = 3 mm
¼ inch = 6 mm
½ inch = 1.5 cm
¾ inch = 2 cm
1 inch = 2.5 cm

OVEN TEMPERATURES

250°F = 120°C
275°F = 140°C
300°F = 150°C
325°F = 160°C
350°F = 180°C
375°F = 190°C
400°F = 200°C
425°F = 220°C
450°F = 230°C

BAKING PAN SIZES

Utensil	Size in Inches/Quarts	Metric Volume	Size in Centimeters
Baking or Cake Pan (square or rectangular)	8×8×2	2 L	20×20×5
	9×9×2	2.5 L	23×23×5
	12×8×2	3 L	30×20×5
	13×9×2	3.5 L	33×23×5
Loaf Pan	8×4×3	1.5 L	20×10×7
	9×5×3	2 L	23×13×7
Round Layer Cake Pan	8×1½	1.2 L	20×4
	9×1½	1.5 L	23×4
Pie Plate	8×1¼	750 mL	20×3
	9×1¼	1 L	23×3
Baking Dish or Casserole	1 quart	1 L	—
	1½ quart	1.5 L	—
	2 quart	2 L	—